▲▼ Going I   Going down to the barrio
homeboy

DATE DUE

Going Down to the Barrio

Homeboys and Homegirls
in Change

Joan W. Moore

 temple university press ▲ **philadelphia**

Temple University Press, Philadelphia 19122
Copyright © 1991 by Temple University.
All rights reserved
Published 1991
Printed in the United States of America

Library of Congress Cataloging-in-Publication Data
Moore, Joan W.
  Going down to the barrio : homeboys and
  homegirls in change / Joan W. Moore.
      p.   cm.
  Includes bibliographical references (p.) and index.
  ISBN 0-87722-854-X (cloth). — ISBN 0-87722-855-8
  (paperback)
  1. Gangs—California—Los Angeles.   2. Mexican
American criminals—California—Los Angeles.   3. Mexican
Americans—California—Los Angeles—Social conditions.
I. Title.
HV6439.U5M66   1991
364.1'06'60979494—dc20   91-2276

▲▼ contents

▲▼ acknowledgments

This book owes a great deal to many people. Robert Garcia gave many years of his life to the research that was carried on by the Chicano Pinto Research Project, the group that he helped found and the group that (under a sanitized name) conducted this research. He was president of the organization for many years and directed the project that collected most of the data reported in this book. In addition, he has been unfailingly generous with his time, his thoughts, and his lifetime expertise in the topics this book attempts to deal with. He has been endlessly patient in his efforts to help me understand not only the details but also the context of the lives we have tried to portray. Without him, this book and its predecessor, *Homeboys*, could not have taken anything like their present form or acquired anything like their value.

I am also indebted to the field research staff of this research project—members of the White Fence and Hoyo Maravilla gangs—for their perseverance and their willingness to share their insights. They include Arturo Ayala, Gus Delgadillo, Robert Esquibel, Hortensia Lagunas, Larry Martinez, Ofelia Moreno, Carmen Ornelas, James Provencio, Rudy Sanchez, and Diana Rodriguez. John Long, as in many other research projects, provided important continuity and colleagueship, as did Diego Vigil, and both helped by giving me access to data from their 1988 study of Irregular Lifestyles. At the University of Wisconsin, Milwaukee, Mary Devitt was endlessly patient and conscientious in helping me work with the computer files.

Michael Backenheimer, the project officer at the National Institute on Drug Abuse who administered the grant (DAO 3114) that funded this research project, went far out of his way to help our group, and I am deeply grateful to him. NIDA, of course, bears no responsibility for the positions taken anywhere in this volume. In the tricky and difficult task of compiling materials on economic restructuring in East Los Angeles, I received considerable help from Rebecca Morales and Paul Ong of the University of California, Los Angeles, and from Marge Nichols of the United Way; I appreciate their assistance.

Finally, I would like to thank my husband, Burton Moore, for his unwavering support over these many years of long-distance commuting-style fieldwork in Los Angeles, and for his creative and invaluable help on this manuscript—as editor, as clarifier for some of the more tangled ideas, and as occasional spot researcher.

Any book is really a collective project, even though it bears a single author's name. This is no exception. In addition to drawing on the cumulated and ongoing work of my fellow academic researchers, I have been privileged to be able to draw on more than fifteen years of research experience with these two gangs. Though the book rests primarily on data from one project, it reflects the findings of many previous studies as well.

▲▼ **Going Down to the Barrio**

homeboys and homegirls in change

chapter one

Introduction

This is a study of two Chicano gangs in East Los Angeles and how they have changed over time. The gangs originated in the 1940s in a climate of hysteria. They continue to operate in a climate of renewed hysteria. American cities are swept by periodic waves of fear and outrage about poor and racially distinctive young men. These outbreaks of fear usually begin with reports from law enforcement people, and are greatly helped along by newspapers and other media and especially by television in recent years. "Moral panic" is perhaps the most useful phrase; it was coined by an English observer of these epidemic affairs (Cohen, 1980).

These moral panics occur periodically, almost by generations. Sometimes the activities that frighten people are defined as "riots" or "rebellions." Black ghettoes erupted in the 1920s, the 1940s, and the 1960s. Hispanics also rioted in the 1960s. Sometimes the fear is generated by gangs. In the 1950s, Los Angeles was terrified by "ratpacks" of Mexican teenagers, and in the late 1980s the nation was swept by a panic about drug-dealing black and Hispanic gangs. When these panics are under way, virtually everything that we learn about what's really happening comes from only two urban institutions—police and media—both with powerful, self-interested motives. The police need recognition and funds; the media need audiences.

Two successive moral panics in the city of Los Angeles are particularly important. One was in the 1940s, and the two gangs we study were part of that scene. The other is contemporary. In both events, the media reported directly as truth and as fact the opinions of the police establishment.[1]

The first moral panic was a response to the famous Zoot-Suit Riots. In

1942, a young Chicano was killed in a gang-related incident now famous as the "Sleepy Lagoon" case. All twenty-two members of a gang were arrested on charges of conspiracy to commit murder. Seventeen of the gang members were convicted. Three were found guilty of first degree murder, nine were found guilty of second degree murder, and five were convicted of other offenses. The newspapers and radio burst into a blare of publicity about the dangers of Mexican zoot-suit gangs. Police began a series of what they called preventive actions. Mostly this meant sweep arrests and dragnet raids, which involved more than six hundred young Chicanos.

In this atmosphere a group of Anglo servicemen on leave in the city got into a series of short but bloody clashes with anybody they defined as gang members. Usually this included zoot-suited Mexican bystanders with no gang involvement whatsoever (Dieppa, 1973:9; Gonzalez, 1981; Mazón, 1985). State and national public opinion condemned the riots as racist. The trial itself was very biased. In fact, by late 1944 all 17 of the Sleepy Lagoon convictions were overturned. But local authorities, and local media, persisted in focusing on gangs as the problem, and specifically as a Mexican problem.

This sudden violent reaction to a group of people who had lived in Los Angeles since the earliest days provoked a great deal of attention. Los Angeles had rioted against Mexicans before (from the earliest days of the city), but now social scientists of the 1940s began to study the zoot-suit gangs quite seriously, asking, in effect, if there *was* anything to fear. Most researchers discounted any serious problems (Bogardus, 1943; McWilliams, 1943). They saw the gangs as typical responses of troubled second-generation youngsters caught up in a tangle of confusion about opportunity and acculturation (see Griffith, 1948). The Chicano gangs of the 1940s were described as very similar to the gangs that had been studied a generation previously, in immigrant Chicago, by Frederick Thrasher (1927). Chicago's gangs disappeared as the immigrant communities were absorbed into the larger economy. Thus it was reasonable to believe that the Chicano gangs would also disappear as matters improved for the Mexican-American population.

In short, it appeared that the zoot-suit panic had very little to do with the violence and criminality of young Mexican-American men, and a lot to do with how Anglos saw Mexicans in Los Angeles. These gangs were *not* to disappear, of course; they are the progenitors of the gangs discussed in this book.

The second moral panic centered on minority gangs of the 1980s. More narrowly, in Los Angeles a series of particularly brutal street shootings by black gangs began a long and intense reaction. The impact was very sharp. In 1977 the *Los Angeles Times* printed only thirty-six stories about gangs; only fifteen were printed in 1978. In 1987, sixty-nine articles appeared, and in 1988 an amazing 267, nearly all of them dealing with police sweeps, revenge shootings, murder trials, and other criminal matters. Nearly all were reports about black gangs, although usually they were not identified as such.[2]

Two particularly dramatic happenings kept gang stories on television every night and in the newspapers almost every day. First, early in 1988, a young woman was shot to death on a busy street in Westwood Village, a rich university community in West Los Angeles. Second, there was a series of massive police sweeps in "gang areas"—mostly in South Central Los Angeles. Most of these events concerned black gangs in black areas, but usually Los Angelenos were left to themselves to decide whether Hispanics or blacks were the victims or the perpetrators. Both the Westwood shooting and the police sweeps raised critical racial questions. An editorial in the *Los Angeles Times* said, "At issue in the growing debate are delicate matters of race, economics and politics, and how Los Angeles' richest and poorest residents see themselves and each other" (January 4, 1988). After the killing of Karen Toshima in Westwood, the city assigned thirty detectives and fourteen foot officers to the case and posted $35,000 in rewards to find her murderer. Both the Hispanic and the black communities complained that no comparable effort was made for gang killings of minority people in poor areas.

The sweeps raised yet other questions. During their most intense phase, the police sweeps (officially coded "The Hammer") lasted four straight weekends with two hundred extra officers on the streets and up to sixteen hundred persons either arrested or cited. The police technique was basically to arrest, cite, or make field reports on every male encountered on the street except those of advanced age. Most of the police activity was directed toward "drug gangs," although the drug-related results were often very small. The first four sweeps of 1988, for example, resulted in 563 arrests (mostly on warrants) and precisely three ounces of cocaine, two pounds of marijuana, and drug-related cash totaling $9,000. The resulting rage in the communities was considerable. There were many charges of police brutality and insensitivity to minority feelings, both Hispanic and black. Some serious depredations were committed by over-enthusiastic officers, including the virtual demolition of an apartment house in South Central Los Angeles, ostensibly while searching for drugs.

Virtually all of the shootings, sweep arrests, and associated bad publicity involved black gangs. The county sheriff, whose jurisdiction covers most of the Chicano gang areas, said he felt no need for sweeps, though an influential county supervisor publicly demanded the use of the National Guard. Some of the black groups were deeply involved in criminal activity. Yet the avoidance of racial labels in the newspapers and the loose and general use of the word "gang" embroiled all gangs, no matter their ethnicity or harmlessness.

In summary: the newspaper reports during 1988 and 1989 in the most conservative newspaper in the city, the *Los Angeles Times*, gave the impression that there was a *continual crisis*. Gang crime was felt to be quite beyond the bounds of any normal latitude for aggressive minority youth. The media felt that strenuous retaliation was justified and, in fact, most Los Angeles citizens told poll-takers that they agreed.

Although it was obvious that black and Hispanic gangs were forming in many smaller cities and many regions of the country, attention centered on Los Angeles. Law-enforcement people began describing Los Angeles as the nation's gang capital. Some claimed that gangs dealing with crack were being franchised in smaller cities in order to establish broad drug-marketing networks.

This series of sensational and often contradictory reports raises considerable doubt about the validity of police and media interpretations. For example, both police and media assumed that the increase in gang-related violence was related to the increase in gang involvement in the sales of cocaine and crack. However, when these assumptions were actually tested with Los Angeles Police Department data for the period from 1983 to 1985, they proved to be wrong (Klein, Maxson, and Cunningham, 1988). Involvement in drug sales of individuals identified as gang members did increase slightly, but the overwhelming majority of individuals arrested in these five South Central stations (75 percent) were *not* gang members. Cocaine may have had a big impact in generating violence but it was not because of gang involvement.

Los Angeles had seen similar misdirected panics before, and there is always some residual effect on legislation, in police practice, and in public opinion. Thus the California state legislature responded from 1984 to 1987 by passing eighty-three separate bills designed to suppress gang activity—and in particular to control alleged drug connections. The laws ranged from new penalties for the operators of drug laboratories (with little effect on street gangs) to greatly increasing the penalty for being under the influence of PCP (with considerable effect on street gang members). In 1989, the state senate passed a law permitting random stop-and-searches for firearms; later that same year the district attorney announced that he would no longer permit plea bargaining for any offense involving gang members. His reasoning: gang members belonged in prison.

Some social scientists used the same framework to interpret the gangs of the 1980s as was used to interpret the gangs of the 1940s. In this view, gangs stem from culturally distinctive populations, and their activities must be explained in light of that cultural distinctiveness (see Horowitz, 1983). In time, of course, this distinctiveness vanishes. Such recent observers may have abandoned their beliefs that Chicanos will become absorbed into the larger society. Still, this cultural interpretation is "optimistic" in its implication that the gangs are nothing much for people to get upset about. Other social scientists view gang activity as reminiscent of the origins of organized crime, and argue that these new gangs foreshadow an evolution of youthful deviance into adult criminality (see Kornblum, 1987). This, indeed was something to be concerned about.[3]

I take a different view of the gang realities behind the 1980s moral panic. I also clearly distinguish between black and Chicano gangs, which developed in very different culture areas of the city. Like many other social scientists I am impressed by the critical changes in the barrios and ghettos over more than forty years—nearly two generations. Of course there is still poverty and there is still a miasmic air of discrimination, less sharp than in the 1940s, perhaps, but definitely a factor in life choices and opportunities. But there appears to be something new—what some have rather controversially called an "underclass"—a kind of *lumpenproletariat,* a stratum of men and women who simply cycle around and around with little if any chance to climb out of the realities of their decayed and defeated neighborhoods. This was the view of William Julius Wilson (1987).

New gangs began to appear in cities that had not seen such phenomena for decades. Nearly always this happened in black and Hispanic communities. In rustbelt cities that had seen good factory jobs disappear, the new gangs were beginning to be seen as part of a growing underclass (Hagedorn, 1988; Huff, 1988). In many communities—like Los Angeles, El Paso, and Chicago—gangs that were established decades earlier had become quasi-institutionalized. For some young men and women the gangs functioned somewhat the way male age groups functioned in some African and Australian tribes studied years ago (Warner, 1937; Wilson, 1951). They developed a clear-cut age stratification, with one clique succeeding another in rather orderly fashion. Each clique had a name and a separate identity. (See Chapter Three for a list of the cliques in the gangs we studied.) At least partially, they helped order adolescents' lives. They provided outlets for sociability, for courtship, and other normal adolescent activities. But they did more: They also tolerated and even encouraged fighting and delinquency (Moore and Vigil, 1987). The legitimate institutions of socialization—family and schools—had become less salient, and "street socialization" (see Vigil, 1988c) began to compete with or supplement the legitimate institutions.

These are the gangs I report on in this book—longstanding Chicano barrio gangs. When these gangs first got started, families were mostly immigrants—like those of Thrasher's 1920s Chicago—and many had difficulty guiding their children through the American experience (see Vigil 1988a). The schools were also marginal. In Thrasher's Chicago, the gangs faded because the populations became absorbed into the larger system. Unfortunately in the communities I studied there were persistent problems in integrating the population into the system as well as continuing immigration from Mexico. This meant that the legitimate institutions remained comparatively marginal and the alternative structure—the gang—could become institutionalized.

As we will see later in much more detail, today's gangs are different from those of the 1940s. Any hope for careers for this generation of young men and women had been drastically curtailed by the disappearance of decent jobs and job ladders. This difference is not confined to Los Angeles. It has serious implications for all American cities. As the institutions ordering the role transitions to young adulthood—work and family—become less salient in changing circumstances, these adolescent quasi-institutions begin to be a focus of the lives of young adults, as well.

It is obvious that moral panics build on exaggerated fears of something "new" in the ghettos and barrios. But let's take the fear seriously for a moment, especially the fear of gangs. Let's assume that what people are afraid of is something that might actually happen. Are the gangs going to develop into new forms of organized crime? Are they going to become revolutionaries? Both of these worries may be disguised forms of racism. It is not possible to deal with either fear unless we have much more of the most basic kind of information; we must also clear up some ambiguities about youth gang members. That is the purpose of this book. Following the data and some new research, I will take a long perspective, measure some changes, and try to decide how much two Chicano youth gangs have changed since the first, well-documented moral panic of the World War II years.

American media grow a little more efficient every generation, so it is not surprising that the most recent panic was national in scope. Otherwise, the most recent panic is very much like the earlier ones. One feature of moral panics is that they seem to involve a rather diffuse fear of all minorities, rather than fear of a single group. In the 1980s, "gangs" were the focus of that fear, and it made no difference to the media that Chicano gangs were very different from black gangs.[4] In fact, there is good reason to believe that, as Thrasher claimed, "all gangs are different" (1927:45). Even within one city, gangs of the same ethnicity behave differently. It is certain that there are major differences from one city to another as well as from one ethnic group to another, and even between gangs of the same ethnic group in the same city.

This book deals with a number of these different interpretations. The focus is on gangs that became quasi-institutionalized over the past forty-odd years in two Chicano barrios in East Los Angeles. Gangs have persisted in these communities since the late 1930s (in El Hoyo Maravilla) and the early 1940s (in White Fence). There may well be observable changes—and they may be important in understanding how gangs impinge on the larger society. These changes may also shed some light on an even more critical question: Are there signs that an underclass is forming in these Chicano communities in large cities?

There is yet the question of data. It is reasonable to assume that adolescent semidelinquents are very difficult to survey and to study. In an earlier study we overcame some of these difficulties by a collaborative effort between academics and ex-offender gang *veteranos,* mostly young or middle-aged men and women. That research group is described in detail in the report of the study (Moore et al., 1978). It had its origin in organizations that reflected the ideals of the Chicano Movement, developing both in prison and in the free world. The original team incorporated itself in 1980 as the Chicano Pinto Research Project with Robert Garcia as president. Under his leadership, research teams were reconstituted for several subsequent projects, including the study reported in this book.

The essence of this collaborative research means that ex–gang member staff are involved at every stage of the research, from design of the interview guide through critical review of written reports.[5] The staff knew—or could locate—gang members from almost any clique. This meant that we were able to create something that is unique in gang research—a random sample of 156 men and women who had been members of these two gangs. We interviewed them in 1985, when they were all adults. It is important to emphasize that we interviewed women as well as men. Gang researchers often neglect female members, but a full third of the sample were female, and this accurately reflects the proportion of girls that were active in the gangs.

Forty percent of our respondents were what we could call "old-timers," those who joined the gang during the late 1940s and early 1950s. The remainder had been active in more recent years—the 1960s and 1970s. Because we talked at length with members from the earliest days of the first cliques up to very recent cliques of these gangs, we know a great deal about their changes and evolution. Those we interviewed were selected randomly from rosters of the 635 original participants in these particular cliques of the gangs. Details on the complex sampling procedure are provided in the appendix.

Behind all these data is an important set of economic and social changes in these two communities between the 1950s and the 1970s. These provide the substantive context for the analysis of changes in the gangs. I describe those changes in Chapter Two. Once done, it will be possible to discuss theoretical issues—and to deal with the concept of the underclass as applied to Hispanics and to gangs. In Chapter Three

I begin this discussion, focusing on the origins, structure, and institutionalization of the gangs. Throughout this and succeeding chapters, I deal consistently with differences between males and females, as well as searching for evidence of change. In Chapter Three I also touch on various ways of interpreting the changes in the gangs during this period. In Chapters Four and Five I deal substantively with these changes, and the extent to which the gangs have become more deviant and more isolated from conventional agents of socialization.

Institutions develop where there are gaps in the existing institutional structure. Gangs as youth groups develop among the socially marginal adolescents for whom school and family do not fill socialization needs. In Chapter Six I discuss the families of these gang members. But gangs persist as young-adult institutions in a changed society, in which the labor market is not filling the needs of the transition from adolescence to young adulthood. It is not that they are rebels, rather it is that they are left out of the credentialed, ordered society. The adult lives of more recent members are quite different in some ways from those of members of earlier cliques, and that is the topic of Chapter Seven.

Finally, we must return to some of the questions we have raised in this introduction. We must not only assess gangs as neighborhood institutions in these communities but we must see how their fate and the fate of their members are also linked to changes in the larger system. And beyond the objective realities, minority gangs continue to symbolize and reaffirm both racial and gender cleavages in this society.

chapter two

The Setting: East Los Angeles

Both of our barrios are small pieces of an area known generally as East Los Angeles. During the entire period of our study Los Angeles and certain surrounding areas housed the largest single concentration of Mexican Americans in this country—a sort of Chicano capital, unmatched anywhere except perhaps in certain areas in Texas. inside this concentration, the White Fence gang lives in a city neighborhood known as Boyle Heights. Just east is the cluster of neighborhoods known as Maravilla, in an unincorporated part of the county known more specifically as East Los Angeles. There are several gangs in Maravilla: The one we studied calls itself El Hoyo Maravilla.

In this chapter I am concerned with the economic and social conditions of these two neighborhoods during the periods when our respondents were actively involved in the gangs. These include the late 1940s and the 1950s, and the late 1960s and the 1970s.

Los Angeles and the Two Neighborhoods in the Early Years

Both of these neighborhoods have a long history, by Los Angeles standards. Boyle Heights (where White Fence emerged) was developed before World War I as an exclusive suburb on the heights east of downtown and across the Los Angeles River. In the 1920s, cheaper housing attracted an extraordinarily heterogeneous population. It was the heart of Los Angeles' Jewish community, and there were also Armenians, Italians, Japanese, and members of a Russian pietistic sect, the Molokans. Mexicans began building shacks in the ravines and hollows (Gustafson,

1940). By the 1940s, this influx meant that Boyle Heights had replaced the downtown Plaza area as the major point of entry for Mexican immigrants to Los Angeles (Acuña, 1984). The Japanese population of Boyle Heights was forced out of the community into detention camps during World War II, and the exodus of the Jewish and Molokan populations accelerated during the 1940s. During the 1930s and 1940s, Boyle Heights looked like an ethnically integrated part of the city, but Mexicans were well on their way to displacing other ethnic groups.

Mexicans appeared in unincorporated East Los Angeles (where the Hoyo Maravilla gang developed) well before the 1920s but the process accelerated with the construction of the Belvedere Gardens development, where a dairy and vegetable farm had once thrived. Often, as in Boyle Heights, Mexicans built self-help housing—shack homes constructed from scrap lumber and salvaged materials. The Maravilla neighborhood of East Los Angeles was heavily Mexican in the 1930s, competing with Boyle Heights as an area of first settlement for immigrants (McWilliams, 1949). In the barrio that housed the gang that we study, El Hoyo (the hole), there was originally no water service, no sewer, no pavement, and no gas main. Water was delivered to the top of a hill, and residents carried it home in buckets. The homes were built in a dry river bed, and in the late 1920s a flash flood swept away houses and drowned residents. Soon after, county authorities filled in the river bed but not until the late 1930s were basic utilities installed (Moore et al., 1978).

In both Boyle Heights and El Hoyo Maravilla, Mexican groceries and restaurants flourished. Mutual-aid societies and other voluntary organizations developed, many with a patriotic Mexican theme focusing on national holidays. Mexicans were very reluctant to take on U.S. citizenship, often feeling that they would not gain much in a discriminatory society and would lose the protections that Mexican citizenship afforded them. The Mexican consulate in Los Angeles served a broad range of functions, often acting as the only advocate available to the population (Balderrama, 1982; Romo, 1983).

During the 1930s, only a minority (18 percent in 1940) of Los Angeles' workers were employed in manufacturing.[1] But there were the seeds of future manufacturing strength. Aircraft and auto-assembly plants were operating, along with tire and auto-parts factories. The garment and furniture industries were solidly in place, and Mexicans were a significant fraction of workers in both industries. (They played a vital part in

Table 2-1. Families by Income Level, Los Angeles and the United States, 1959

Income level	Los Angeles	Boyle Heights	East L.A.	United States
Poverty (Under $4,000)	19.1%	35.6%	29.6%	30.9%
Deprivation ($4,000–$5,999)	19.1	27.2	28.5	23.3
Deprivation-Comfort ($6,000–$7,999)	21.6	19.4	20.8	19.3
Comfort ($8,000–$14,999)	32.4	16.4	19.5	21.7
Affluence ($15,000 and over)	7.8	1.4	1.6	4.8

Source: Meeker with Harris, 1964:49, xxxvii.

major garment strikes in 1933 and 1936, for example). Mexicans were also working in food-processing plants, brick and clay factories, metals plants, and printing and paper plants as well as railroads, restaurants, and other service industries. Except for aircraft, rubber, and auto factories, most plants in the Los Angeles area were small.

After World War II, when these two gangs were becoming established, Los Angeles enjoyed a spectacular postwar boom. Manufacturing had expanded greatly during the war, and, in spite of a short postwar recession (1948–1949), it continued to expand well into the late 1950s. One and a half million people were added to the county by 1960, and almost two million more arrived during the next decade. Orange groves, bean fields, and market gardens were giving way to huge tracts of housing to accommodate the newcomers. Money was being made: Los Angeles had an astonishing proportion of rich people compared with the rest of the country (see Table 2-1).

The boom bypassed Boyle Heights and Maravilla, leaving these neighborhoods still very poor. Conditions were improving in both communities, but both were part of an expanding poverty pocket. Compared with the rest of Los Angeles' 134 community areas, these two neighborhoods ranked in the bottom 10 percent for income and education and the top 10 percent for population density.[2] Unemployment rates were well above the average for the county as a whole (Meeker, 1964).

Even though Mexican Americans constituted no more than 60 percent of either neighborhood, Boyle Heights and East Los Angeles were seen by the rest of Los Angeles as the "Mexican" part of town. (Actually it was not until 1970 that the area became overwhelmingly Mexican.) Small lots and large families made these two communities among the most densely populated in the county. In a city in which more than half of the residents owned their own homes, fewer than a third of the Boyle Heights residents and only 41 percent of those living in unincorporated East Los Angeles owned their homes in 1960 (Meeker, 1964). Rentals—almost all for single-family houses—were among the cheapest in the county, and by 1960 East Los Angeles had "the greatest concentration of poor housing" in the county (Meeker, 1964:34). Welfare rates were high. So were infant death rates as well as death rates from every major communicable disease (U.S. Dept. of Commerce, 1965:40). In general, in the mid 1950s, delinquency rates for Mexican-American (and black) boys were about triple those for Anglos (Eaton and Polk, 1961).[3] Despite these objective indicators of misery, the communities seemed to be reasonably strong, with a considerable sense of community pride.

The Los Angeles economy continued to flourish during the 1950s. Manufacturing grew—from only 29 percent of all employment in 1950 to more than 36 percent by the middle of the decade (California, 1989). Not only was there an increased demand for consumer goods, but the machines and weapons of war were needed to sustain the cold war and the Korean conflict. The defense industry—the aerospace industry in particular—began to dominate manufacturing, supplying almost 40 percent of its employment.

Much of the boom was based on a change from the simple production of airplanes to sophisticated aerospace, missile, and electronic technology. This involved a rapid shift from skilled to professional labor.[4] Thus by the late 1950s Los Angeles was already beginning a pattern that became familiar in the "postindustrial" 1980s—increasing proportions of professional and clerical workers and declining proportions of blue-collar workers. Skilled production workers were suffering from unemployment, but there was a shortage of engineers and technicians (Meeker, 1964:43–46). Chicanos and other minorities were largely excluded from these excellent new jobs. Even if they had been qualified, aerospace plants were located many miles from the East Los Angeles barrios.[5]

Mexicans had been able to find good jobs in aircraft and ship building during the labor shortages of World War II. But they lost ground in the high-paying defense industry after the war (Greer, 1959).[6] Nonetheless, Mexicans *were* being hired in other expanding sectors of manufacturing. Notably, these included large-scale auto assembly, tire, auto parts, and steel plants located on the edge of East Los Angeles. Garment, shoe, and furniture factories were also important as were vegetable packing and other food processing, especially in the slaughterhouses and cattle pens near downtown. They also continued to work in the citrus groves and market gardens that edged East Los Angeles.

The early bifurcation of work in Los Angeles County meant that although there were comparatively many more well-off and affluent—and fewer poor—families in Los Angeles than in the nation as a whole, the families in East Los Angeles and Boyle Heights were concentrated in the bottom income categories (Table 2-1).[7] Residential segregation massed the minority populations into ghettos (like Watts) and extensive clusters of Mexican-American barrios (like East Los Angeles).

But we must also consider political issues as well as economic factors. Greater East Los Angeles was not simply a reservoir of poor Mexican laborers, as one cynical historian viewed it (Acuña, 1984). Political organization had been present even during the 1930s, though at very low levels (Garcia, 1985), and often with a genuflection in the direction of the Mexican origins of so many of the adult residents. After World War II, however, when U.S.–born young men came back from military service, political activity accelerated. After some unsuccessful trial runs, Edward Roybal was elected to the Los Angeles City Council—the first person of Mexican origin to serve since the nineteenth century. Roybal was a lone voice on the city council for many of the issues that concerned his East Los Angeles constituents.

Several issues, some quite blatant and others rather more subtle, combined to encourage political participation in East Los Angeles after the war. First, there were several "land grabs" (Acuña, 1984). Initially they centered around the construction of the freeways radiating east from downtown.[8] At the beginning of the 1950s, only eleven miles of freeway were operational, but in the next ten years an additional two hundred miles were added. Two of these freeways (the San Bernardino and Santa Ana) cut through the heart of East Los Angeles barrios, and in the next decade two more freeways were to wipe out even larger areas. Both of the neighborhoods we study were greatly affected. A tract in one of the barrios actually lost 60 percent of its population in the 1950s. Community myth held that the freeway was deliberately designed to cut through the neighborhood and thereby break up the gang. Homeowners and merchants were upset both at the destruction of neighborhoods and at the low prices paid for properties. East Los Angeles is now crisscrossed by no less than four freeways. The resulting noise and air pollution is considered a permanent detriment, even though local merchants like the quick access to their businesses.

A second factor concerned the youth problems discussed in Chapter One. These problems became newsworthy with the trial of the twenty-two defendants in the 1942 Sleepy Lagoon case, and they continued to be a focus of Mexican-American political concern. From the very beginning, residents resented the stigmatizing coverage in the highly prejudiced media. The protest about the Sleepy Lagoon case was led by Anglo liberals (who were thoroughly red-baited) but East L. A. residents took note when the convictions of seventeen of the defendants was overturned a year later by the District Court of Appeals. The court criticized both the prosecution and the trial judge for conducting a biased trial (González, 1981; Morales, 1972). The Zoot-Suit Riots also prompted East Los Angeles youth-service organizations to send a strong protest to federal authorities at the way in which local newspapers were inflaming public opinion (Garcia, 1985).

The city continued to be barraged with sensationalist newspaper publicity about the so-called dangers posed by Chicano youth well into the 1950s, and there were more widespread protests in East Los Angeles. The Saul Alinsky–inspired Community Service Organization, founded in 1947, was in the forefront of many of these protests. In 1950 after the release of some boys who had been arrested in a so-called ratpack attack, the *Eastside Sun* charged that the mainstream newspapers were using "scare headlines which are similar to those that threw us into a 'zoot-suit' riot in 1943. . . . We do not condone the lawlessness of a degraded metropolitan press that helps in this campaign of falsehood in order to reap profits" ("Who Are the Wolf Packs?" *Eastside Sun*, May 18, 1950, p. 1). Three years later, Ralph Guzman, a journalist who was to become the first Chicano political scientist, wrote in the same paper: "Today our Eastside community is again a scapegoat. It has been abused, vilified and condemned by newspapers with reckless editorial policies, public officials sick with personal prejudices, and well meaning but confused civic leaders. Narcotics, youth gang warfare, sadistic crimes, drunken brawls and all manner of crime have been attributed to the one part of the city that does not object—the Eastside!" (*Eastside Sun*, June 25, 1953, p. 1).

And six months later he continued to complain: "When teenagers in other parts of the city go astray, the newspapers call it juvenile delinquency, but when Eastside kids wander from the straight and narrow they are immediately tagged as 'Rat-Packs,' 'Mad Dogs,' and 'Bloodthirsty Hoodlums' " (*Eastside Sun*, December 17, 1953, p. 1).

Police prejudice and brutality were related issues helping politicize East Los Angeles. For decades, both city police and county sheriff's officials delivered racist "explanations" to account for Mexican-American youth problems—always accompanied by a storm of protest from the community. For decades, organized labor—Mexican-American locals, in particular—joined with Mexican-American civic organizations and the Community Service Organization (CSO) in protests against police brutality (Acuña, 1981). Between 1948 and 1954, the CSO conducted thirty-five investigations into police brutality against Mexican Americans. This included the "Bloody Christmas" case, one of the extremely rare instances in which Los Angeles police officers were disciplined.[9]

However strong the grievances, and however real the politicization, East Los Angeles did not win substantial political representation on any level—city, county, or state—until many years later.

The Two Neighborhoods in Later Years

In the 1980s a number of significant changes took place in these communities. Yet in some fundamental ways there were no changes at all.

In 1980, as in earlier years, there was a continuing influx of immigrants and exodus of second-generation Chicanos to outlying areas. The two communities were still very poor, with more than a third of the population in poverty, compared with less than a fifth of the county as a whole.[10] People still lagged far behind in educational attainment: At a time when Los Angeles' residents completed on the average one year of college, residents of these two Eastside communities averaged only eight years of elementary school.

Housing was old. In the county as a whole, only a third of the housing was older than thirty years, but the proportion rose to two-thirds in these two Eastside communities. While 45 percent of the county's dwelling units were owner-occupied, only a quarter of the units in Boyle Heights and a third of the units in unincorporated East Los Angeles were owned by their residents. Overwhelmingly, this was a community of renters, living largely in older homes. Often these houses were owned by people who had lived in them as youngsters, and inherited them from their parents (TELACU, 1978). In most of Los Angeles County, the price of housing had skyrocketed. But in these communities, housing was still cheaper and more affordable; thus fewer people were paying large portions of their income for rent.

Two changes were causing problems. First, there was an upsurge of immigration, and second, there were shifts in the quality of available jobs. On the positive side, Mexican Americans in these communities for the first time were winning substantial political representation.

The 1970s and 1980s saw a dramatic increase in immigration from Mexico to Los Angeles County (McCarthy and Valdez, 1986; Muller and Espenshade, 1986; Ong, 1988). As always, Boyle Heights and East Los Angeles were ports of entry for many immigrants. In 1980 the census recorded that 45 percent of the adults in Boyle Heights and 38 percent in East Los Angeles spoke no English at all. These proportions increased in the early 1980s. Historically, ecological succession in American cities meant that a wave of new immigrants displaces an older group of different ethnicity. Over the decades, Mexicans seem to have enacted a version of this same scenario that is less traceable because the displacement is *intra*-ethnic. New waves of Mexican immigrants have continued to settle in poor Mexican barrios, as those barrios were vacated by upwardly mobile residents. This is indeed an exodus, but it tends to involve only some of the children of stable working-class people who remain in the barrio.

The influx meant that the two communities continued to be very poor. In some ways, these new immigrants did not much affect the lives of those Chicanos remaining in the communities. These barrios always had been poor and Spanish always had been common. That there were more monolingual Spanish speakers than before did not matter. And, in fact, many of the new immigrants were so highly motivated that their poverty did not seem so demoralizing.

But immigration *did* make a difference in several respects. For one, schools were under much heavier pressure to provide adequate bilingual education in a climate of general reluctance to spend money on education.[11] And for another, more immigrants meant that there was inevitably a serious dilution in the voting strength of these communities. Mexicans have never been eager to become naturalized (Pachon, 1985). Many of the new immigrants lacked the documentation that would *ever* permit them to become eligible for citizenship, even under the amnesty provisions of the new immigration legislation of the mid-1980s.

The most important effect of the large-scale new immigration, however, was that it coincided with local economic restructuring. Thus it worked to drastically constrict the job opportunities available to Chicanos in the area. Manufacturing employment peaked at 36 percent of the labor force during the mid-1950s. By 1975 it had dropped substantially; only a quarter of the working population were employed in manufacturing jobs. But during the 1970s, even more than other Sunbelt boom towns, Los Angeles experienced a major expansion in good jobs in aerospace and high-tech manufacturing and also in the financial and managerial sectors associated with the city's emerging "Pacific Rim" dominance. Paradoxically, the city simultaneously saw "an almost Detroit-like decline of traditional, highly unionized heavy industry," along with an expansion of very low-wage manufacturing and service jobs (see Soja, Morales, and Wolff, 1984:211ff.). Between 1970 and 1980 the total proportion employed in manufacturing dropped by 3 percent (California, 1989), but low-wage manufacturing jobs accounted for 53 percent of the city's growth in employment. Moderate-wage jobs accounted for only 7 percent and high-wage manufacturing for 11 percent (McCarthy and Valdez, 1986:40).[12]

As with the expansion of "good" jobs in the 1940s and 1950s, these new factories and white-collar developments of the 1970s generally excluded minorities (Lane, 1975). By contrast, the decline in traditional manufacturing had a major impact—especially on the communities we studied. The heavily unionized steel and auto industries that were located nearby all but vanished: Auto assembly plants, tire factories, and steel plants that had provided good jobs to workers in the greater East Los Angeles area were no longer in existence.[13]

Further, the expansion of nonunionized, poor-paying jobs in manufacturing and service industries (e.g., restaurants and hotels) also had a major impact on Mexican Americans. Many of the newest immigrants from Mexico and Central America were undocumented, adding to what some authors have called "perhaps the largest pool of cheap, manipulable, and easily dischargeable labor of any advanced capitalist city" (Soja,

Morales, and Wolff, 1984:219). Hispanics filled virtually all of the new jobs created in manufacturing during the decade.[14] And by the end of the decade, the earnings of Hispanics in Los Angeles County had, on the average, declined rather substantially by comparison with Hispanics elsewhere in the nation (McCarthy and Valdez, 1986:44).

Manufacturing jobs continued to be extremely important for Mexican Americans. By 1980, more than a third of U.S.–born Mexican Americans and almost half of all immigrant Mexicans in the county were employed in manufacturing (Morales and Ong, 1988:31). Even among teenagers, Mexican Americans were overrepresented in manufacturing jobs. Because of this dependence, it is especially notable that their presence in traditional manufacturing with good, unionized jobs declined between 1970 and 1980, and their presence in nondurable manufacturing—the low-wage sector—increased.[15]

What was true for Mexican Americans in the county as a whole was also true for Boyle Heights and unincorporated East Los Angeles. In 1980, almost 45 percent of all workers in Boyle Heights and East Los Angeles were employed in manufacturing. Anyone who knows these areas might expect this result. Boyle Heights, for example, is just across the river from Central Los Angeles, and within easy commuting distance of the expanding garment industry. Unincorporated East Los Angeles is immediately adjacent to the City of Commerce, which was originally developed to be an industrial center.[16]

The City of Commerce had been the home of several "good," traditional industries—primary metal, metal working, and paper, in particular. But even in 1970 such firms were beginning to leave the area. In 1968 there were 1,014 manufacturing firms in the area, and by 1972 the number had dropped to 914 and by 1978 to only 761—a 25 percent decline (TELACU, 1978). Of the 565,000 jobs in the City of Commerce, residents of unincorporated East Los Angeles held only 12 percent (Carr et al., 1985). Ironically, one of the complaints of firms leaving the area was that they could not find enough *skilled* workers in East Los Angeles. Equally ironically, some of the firms relocated to Mexico, in search of even cheaper labor (Morales, 1985).[17]

Unemployment generally tended to be somewhat higher in these Eastside communities than in the county as a whole. (In 1980, it hovered around 10 percent, as compared with 6 percent for the county.) Chicanos appear to be more vulnerable to even minor economic downturns (Ong,

1988). But a more serious problem was that so many people were working and were still poor. This was a national pattern: Higher proportions of Mexican Americans who work full-time are below the poverty level.[18] Immigration and economic shifts may have been the most important new problems in East Los Angeles between the 1950s and 1970s, but there were other major changes. During the 1960s, the War on Poverty and the Model Cities programs had generated a number of community-based organizations. These organizations dealt with employment and training, with health, with undocumented immigrants, and with other sorely neglected community needs. Programs for teenaged dropouts, for gang kids, for heroin users, and for ex-offenders and their families were a significant part of this development. Despite setbacks, many were still in place during the 1970s, and others—like the development organization TELACU (The East Los Angeles Community Union)—were also flourishing.[19] Bilingual education was becoming a reality in the elementary schools, and local community colleges were initiating Chicano studies programs as well as special programs for ex-offenders. Tangible construction projects appeared—a new cultural center, a new health center, a new addition to an old housing project.

Political activity in East Los Angeles accelerated during the 1960s and 1970s as the Chicano movement swept the community. There was a series of demonstrations, some marked by violence, against the indifference of the Catholic church, against practices in the school system, against police brutality, against U.S. involvement in Vietnam, and against the excessive number of Chicano casualties in that conflict. At one of these rallies, the police killed a noted Chicano journalist, Ruben Salazar. There was a major outcry at every level of the government at what was seen as just one in a series of flagrant violations of justice. A series of court cases attacked discrimination against Mexican Americans in the Los Angeles grand juries, which had been responsible for indicting many of the militants involved in these demonstrations.

Throughout much of this period, Councilman (later Congressman) Edward Roybal was the sole elected official representing the needs of the East Los Angeles area (or indeed of Chicanos anywhere in Los Angeles County). Roybal took a very strong advocacy role in the events of the turbulent 1960s and 1970s. He began to be joined by other elected officials. Chicanos were elected to the Los Angeles school board, and to the state assembly. But access to the powerful county supervisors was confined to a Chicano "representative" of a supervisor whose constituency also included wealthy Beverly Hills. After Roybal left the city council for Congress, it was not until the 1980s that East Los Angeles could elect another Chicano to the Los Angeles City Council.

The community-based organizations began to fade during the 1970s, even though the problems had not disappeared. In particular, programs for high school dropouts, for gang youth, for ex-offenders and their families, and for heroin addicts vanished. (See Moore, 1985, and Moore et al., 1978, about the origins and dissolution of some of these programs.)

Many of the gains of the 1960s and early 1970s were solidly in place. There was a strong electoral base and the Chicano movement had left an enduring legacy—its accomplishments and ideals were still espoused by men and women now in mainstream institutions. In Chapter One I discussed the Los Angeles panic about gangs in the 1940s and the 1980s. The uproar about Chicano gangs in the 1940s clearly had an effect in East Los Angeles. There were programs in place for the gangs of the 1950s that we study. (See discussion of gang programs in Chapter Three.) Even twenty years later, during the War on Poverty, there was enough residual concern so that both gang and ex-offender programs were still a priority. By the end of the 1970s, however, these programs had disappeared. The gang panic of the 1980s had no programmatic repercussions in East Los Angeles.

Summary and Implications

In the 1980s, economic and social conditions were not good for poorly educated, native-born Chicanos still living in East Los Angeles. This included most of the gang members and their families. Compared with gang men and women a generation earlier, these people were facing much stiffer competition (from large numbers of exploitable and highly motivated immigrants) for jobs that were less and less attractive. Even though the post–World War II boom was echoed only faintly in East Los Angeles, Chicanos in those 1950s communities—including gang members—had been able to get unionized jobs in large firms, and to move up as they acquired seniority. There was a sense of progress: People were moving ahead compared with the immigrant generation of the 1930s. In the 1960s, with the Chicano movement, the injuries and ethnic slights of the earlier generation surfaced and a great sense of empowerment swept through the community.

Good jobs had largely vanished by the time we did our interviewing. They had been replaced by jobs that had low wages, little security, no fringe benefits, and no future. And, even though political representation was solidly in place, the euphoria of the "movement" days had vanished. So had many of the community-based programs generated by the War on Poverty, including programs aimed at gang members.

In the 1970s East Los Angeles was poor compared with the rest of Los Angeles, and it had been throughout the preceding thirty years. Most Chicanos who were able to leave the community did so, leaving a residue of elderly and of poor and uneducated young people, and making room for a vast influx of immigrants eager to take advantage of any opening in the system. The combined effect of increased immigration and economic restructuring had implications not only for young adults, but also for children in East Los Angeles. By the 1980s, the population of East Los Angeles was overwhelmingly of Mexican origin, but the native-born were not necessarily the most advantaged. Clearly some were still doing well in school and at work, but the social structure had changed so that the young men and women who joined the gangs had far less chance to find the kind of work that would encourage them to cut loose their adolescent ties.

chapter three

Two Barrio Gangs: Growth, Structure, and Theoretical Considerations

In this chapter I introduce the two gangs that we have studied, White Fence and El Hoyo Maravilla. I discuss the earliest, founding cliques and then turn to the question of how the gangs became institutionalized within their neighborhoods and what have been the major turning points in their fifty-year history. Brief attention is paid to the parallel history of gang programs—responses to the various moral panics that the gangs have inspired. Finally, I discuss the alternative theoretical perspectives that may make sense out of the changes that are more fully detailed in succeeding chapters.

The Early Days: The Founding Cliques

In the earliest years of the gangs, in the 1930s and 1940s, neighbors in White Fence and El Hoyo Maravilla appear to have defined the male groups not as gangs, but simply as "the boys from the barrio." According to one of the first members of White Fence: "Well, the people in the community, the original gang members, they were the parents, neighbors, families that settled that neighborhood. They all came there from Mexico. Their fathers and mothers knew everybody in the neighborhood. They were all one big community. . . . They didn't consider me as a gang member. Like when I walked down the street, I used to say, 'Hello, so-and-so'; she didn't say, 'Hey this guy is a gang member from White Fence.' No, he's the son of Mrs. M., or the son of so-and-so."

And one of the first members of Hoyo Maravilla commented: "Well at that time they never considered it to be a gang. It was just a meeting of youngsters in the streets. At that time it wasn't considered a gang, not as far as I'm concerned. It was just that you go out and you hang out in the playground or in the street and talk."

It was during the 1920s that Mexican neighborhoods first began to see male groups that sociologists called "gangs" (Bogardus, 1926), but which were more in the Mexican tradition of male barrio groups documented as far back as the nineteenth century (Redfield, 1941). Young males from these barrios hung out together and fought with boys from other barrios at dances and parties, but by adulthood they left the gang. Similar groups, called *palomillas*, appeared in rural Texas (Rubel, 1965) and continued in American cities, attached to specific neighborhoods or barrios as in Mexican cities. The gangs we studied in Los Angeles grew from this traditional base. When a White Fence man was asked about his parents' reaction to the gang, his answer reflects this perception: "My mother? They didn't have no reaction. I was born there; that was the neighborhood. We were part of life there. The gang was the neighborhood."

In White Fence the predecessor of the gang was the young men's sports group organized in the 1930s and associated with La Purissima church. This church was the focus of community life during the 1930s and 1940s. The "Purissima crowd" of boys and young men were fully integrated into community activities. Mixed in age, they were the older brothers and cousins of the boys who were to start the White Fence gang. The same man recalls: "Ah, hell, I looked up to them. . . . There were no drugs at that time, you know, not heavy drugs, and they dressed good and they were very family-oriented. They were the pride of the neighborhood, although they still had their reputation. But in 1941, when the war broke out, they all were drafted."

It was toward the end of World War II—while the stabilizing Purissima crowd was still away at the war—that the White Fence gang got started. (See Table 3–1 for a listing of all cliques in these two gangs between 1935 and 1975.) White Fence was a newcomer gang in East Los Angeles, an area that was already full of youth gangs. The more established gangs at the time considered White Fence to be quite violent (see Moore et al., 1978, for details). They even had the temerity to fight older boys from other gangs, like the Veteranos from El Hoyo Maravilla. (The "Veteranos" are the original clique in any barrio, although the term veterano generally refers to older men in any gang who have been through prison.) The Maravilla neighborhood had some half-dozen gangs, including Arizona Maravilla, Kern Maravilla, Ford Maravilla, and Marianna Maravilla as well as El Hoyo Maravilla. Most of these were named after streets, and each territory was quite small, reflecting barrios packed tightly, one next to the other. (El Hoyo Maravilla is located in a broad arroyo [dry river bed]. The word *hoyo* means hole.) The first clique of the Hoyo Maravilla gang crystallized during the late 1930s, at the same time as the White Fence Purissima crowd. Like the Purissima boys, the clique was actively involved in sports, and, in fact, the two neighborhoods competed against each other in organized games. In the early 1940s a group of gang members started a softball team—the Gophers—and, as in a number of other gangs at the time, several members went in for professional boxing.[1]

The early Hoyo Maravilla gang appears to have been somewhat more like a modern gang than the church-based Purissima crowd. They were pachucos (zoot-suiters) and Maravilla was one of the neighborhoods invaded by marauding servicemen in the brief but vicious Zoot-Suit Riots of 1941. The gang boys fought back; they had a tradition of fighting one-on-one with rival gang members at parties and dances.

As they grew older, the Maravilla gang men began to hang around the local cantinas (beer bars) rather than the church. Yet beach parties, dances, and social functions arranged by the Catholic Youth Organization punctuated their lives in the early 1940s, much as the church picnics marked the lives of the Purissima youth.

In both White Fence and El Hoyo Maravilla, the older boys went off to World War II. This abrupt departure created sharp discontinuities for the boys who remained to carry on neighborhood traditions.

What about the girls? The literature on girl gangs is very thin (see Campbell, 1984; Harris, 1988; Quicker, 1983). Much of it assumes that girl gangs are "auxiliaries" that are tightly bound to boys' cliques. But in the late 1930s and early 1940s the girls' gangs in Maravilla were not only *not* tightly bound to boy's cliques but they were also much less bound to particular barrios than the boys'. The Black Legion, the Cherries, the Elks, the Black Cats, and the Vamps were small groups of girls—school friends and relatives. Most claimed no linkage to any specific gang out of the many gangs in the neighborhoods in Maravilla. The girls partied with

Table 3-1. Names and Beginning and Ending Dates for Gang Cliques

Hoyo Maravilla	Dates	White Fence	Dates
"Originals"	1935–1945	*"Originals"	1944–1952
Cherries	1939–1950	*Honeydrippers (girls)	
Vamps[a] (girls)	?	*Monsters	1946–1954
Jive Hounds	1943–1953	*Lil White Fence (girls)	
Lil Cherries	1945–1954	Cherries	1947–1960
*Cutdowns	1946–1956	WF Cherries (girls)	
*Jr. Vamps (girls)		Tinies	1949–1961
*[Big] Midgets	1950–1955	Spiders	1953–1960
Lil Cutdowns	1951–1969	Chonas (girls)	
Las Cutdowns (girls)		Midgets	1957–1966
Penguins	1954–1960	Peewees	1960–?
Lil Midgets	1958–1965	Los Termites	1964–1970
*Las Monas (girls)[b]		Lil Cherries	1964–?
Dukes	1958–1966	*Monstros	1968–?
Tinies	1958–1963	*Monstras (girls)	1970
Santos	1960–1963	*Lil Termites	1972–1981
Peewees	1961–?	*Lil Termites (girls)	
*Locos	1964–1968	Locos	1973–1981
*Las Locas (girls)		Lil Locas (girls)	
*Chicos	1967–?	Lil Spiders	1974–1981
*Las Chicas (girls)		Winitos	1974–1976
Ganzos	1969–?		
*Las Ganzas (girls)			
Jokers	1970–?		
Cyclones	1973–?		
Las Cyclonas (girls)			

*Indicates cliques chosen for sampling.

[a] Most of the Vamps lived in El Hoyo Maravilla, which counts them as one of their cliques, even though they were not formally attached either to the neighborhood or to any boys' clique.

[b] Las Monas was an independent girls clique, contemporaneous with but not an auxiliary of the Lil Midgets, the Dukes, and the Tinies. At the outset of our study we believed that it was attached to the [Big] Midgets. See Appendix for details.

boys from several of these gangs—often with cliques of boys that were
several years older. While new male cliques started every three to five
years in Hoyo Maravilla, the girls' cliques were not so clearly age-graded
and girls from any given clique tended to date boys from several of the
male cliques.

In El Hoyo, not until the mid-1940s and the formation of the Junior
Vamps was there something close to a female auxiliary (allied to the Cutdowns clique). Many of these girls had older sisters in the Vamps and the
Black Cats. Yet the tradition of female autonomy continued in this barrio
with the next clique (Las Monas) forming quite autonomously in the late
1950s. Las Monas started with just a couple of girls who hung around a
local hot-dog stand: "First me and Isabel, and then China said that she
wanted to be a Mona. . . . I guess the guys started naming us that—
the Monas."

But even the girls from the Junior Vamps and Las Monas—the two
earlier cliques that we sampled—dated boys from several cliques and
were not exclusively the allies or "property" of any one male clique.
Several of the Junior Vamps were from families with traditions of gang
involvement and street life.

Girls from White Fence were more like the stereotyped notion of girl
gangs. In that gang it was clear from the beginning that the girls related
to one particular clique of boys, even though they (like the girls of El
Hoyo) were first and foremost a group of friends. We interviewed women
from the Honeydrippers and Lil White Fence—the first two cliques.
The Honeydrippers was named after a black rhythm-and-blues band and
were attached to the original White Fence boys. The sister of one of the
founding boys recalled:

> We started it, me and Pelona and Maggie and India, just hanging
> around together and meeting in each other's house. More girls
> started coming over and then the boys started naming us "Honey-
> drippers." Cause we used to have this record that we used to play
> over and over and over, and they said, "Eee como man, yous play
> that record too much." We loved it. [Was it by the Honeydrippers?]
> Yes. We were learning to dance with the Honeydrippers. Joe Liggins
> and the Honeydrippers. We used to dance in Maggie's house, on the
> porch, because her mother used to let us hang around on her porch.
> She said, "You could hear the records all you want as long as you

behave." So the best one we had to dance to was the Honeydrippers, so we'd put it on and just practice and practice. So the boys would say, "There they go with that song again." So after a while the boys named us the Honeydrippers.

I felt proud because all my brothers—well Moto was in there, and Al—and all the boys, they were always in my back yard with my brother. And the girls were all together. We were neighbors, so I was proud of them.

Most of them were relatives, rather than girlfriends: "Oh yeah, [the boys] took care of us. They always had their eye on us all the time. Cause we were all brothers and sisters there in the neighborhood. They always watched us. . . . But we never went with [dated] the guys from White Fence, let me tell you. They were too much lovers for us." The girls attached to the next boys' clique, the Monsters, called themselves Lil White Fence. They were a small clique and had to call on both the boys and the older Honeydrippers for help in fights:

There wasn't that many girls our age, you know, that wanted to be involved in White Fence. So we had sort of like a dry period where we had to ask the guys, you know, to back us up sometimes, if there was any fights against other barrios. . . . You know when Lola from Varrio Nuevo [rival gang] was after me, Timber [from the Honeydrippers] came to my rescue—her and her friends. And she said, "If you find yourself in trouble come to me." And nobody messed with Timber because that's why they called her Timber.

But not every boys' clique in White Fence had a female counterpart. As in Maravilla, the White Fence girls' cliques were considerably smaller than the boys'. The girls from the Honeydrippers were generally "good" girls. One woman, who had led a completely conventional life except for a brief marriage to a gang member, commented: "Well, I don't know. We weren't bad kids or anything. I can't remember doing anything that I was ashamed of or anything."

However, there are indications in our interviews that the girls who joined the gang (apart from the sisters of male members) tended to be from somewhat more troubled backgrounds than those of the boys (see Chapter Six). Certainly in the 1940s when these early cliques were formed, a Chicana girl seen hanging around on the streets (let alone joining a gang) would prompt name-calling and charges of all kinds of wrongdoing. No matter how innocent their activities, these girls were considered deviant by the neighborhood.

Gang Structure: The Development of a Quasi-institution

The gangs started out as friendship groups of adolescents who shared common interests, with a more or less clearly defined territory in which most of the members lived. They were committed to defending one another, the barrio, the families, and the gang name in the status-setting fights that occurred in school and on the streets. They were bound by a norm of loyalty.

The gangs rapidly developed an age-graded structure and became a quasi-institutionalized agent of socialization—an institutionalized peer group. As the boys of the founding clique matured, some of them got married and settled down, generally tending to drop their ties with the gang. Girls left even earlier—usually when they got pregnant. Others, usually the least stable, remained involved in the street life-style. But the communities were still poor and marginalized and the gangs were still very attractive to boys and girls in the neighborhoods. Clearly, the original members—now in their late teens and early 20s—didn't have much in common with the 13- and 14-year-old boys who clamored for admission. Soon those younger kids formed their own named clique. In White Fence, one of the original members remembers how the next clique— with the intimidating name of "the Monsters" got its name: "Bobo [from the Veteranos] is the one that named them the Monsters. Because all the guys from White Fence [the Veteranos], they were already quite a bit older, and then all the smaller guys—Lugger and all those guys, they were coming on all bad. Bobo said, 'Eee, here come the Monsters. They're *bad*.' And they stayed with that name."

By the end of World War II, the male gangs of East Los Angeles had already developed an age-graded structure, with several named, age-graded cliques. This was the beginning of institutionalization. The White Fence Monsters, formed in 1946, were followed by the Cherries (1947) and the Tinies (1949). In El Hoyo Maravilla, the Veteranos were followed in 1939 by the Cherries, in 1943 by the Jive Hounds, in 1945 by the Lil Cherries, in 1946 by the Cutdowns, and in 1950 by the Midgets.

Many of these cliques were active on the streets at the same time. The original White Fence clique, the Veteranos, did not dissolve until 1952 and the Monsters not until 1954. As many as four cliques were active in the neighborhood at the same time. Each had a separate identity, but each was part of the larger gang. "The neighborhood" or "the barrio" was the first locus of loyalty: it is no coincidence that both terms refer equally to the gang and to the geographical neighborhood. The clique was the closer friendship group within the barrio.

The four cliques active during the late 1940s and early 1950s comprised our sample of earlier cliques. The gangs of this era might be viewed as transitional. Although violent barrio warfare was becoming endemic and costing many injuries and a continuous fire of newspaper publicity, the gangs still had many linkages to conventional groups. White Fence no longer carried the Purissima church banner, but the gang was still involved in sports competitions. Although they won a basketball trophy, the changed image is measured by the fact that they were not permitted to wear their jackets in high school: "I came to Roosevelt High School for one semester—Midnight and I—and since we had won that championship in basketball we had jackets that said 'White Fence' but they wouldn't let us wear it. Everybody else's social club wore their jackets, but they wouldn't let us wear ours. They knew we were gang members. Of course we weren't the only gang in school!"

At about the same time, during the late 1940s, heroin was first used by gang members. This was a major turning point in the development of the gangs. Heroin became especially popular among the older members in Hoyo Maravilla, and the barrio became a center for heroin marketing. Secret federal grand jury indictments secured by undercover agents sent a number of young adult Hoyo Maravilla gang members to prison for the first time in 1950. State laws also became more punitive. Although heroin addiction and prison rarely involved the younger teenagers in the gang, significant fractions began to drop into the heroin subculture in their late teens and early 20s, forever changing the process of maturing out of the gang. Even more important, the larger gang subculture began to incorporate mythologies about coping in prison, and these stories became part of gang tradition for young active members.

Thus the four earlier cliques that we studied were active during a period of transition from an accepted barrio group to something on the far reaches of tolerability. The term "outlaw" was never an accurate term for the gangs we study. Yet it is clear that the gangs of the 1970s were distinctly more deviant than the earlier cliques.

We also chose four cliques that had been active in more recent years—the 1960s and 1970s. Between the founding "Veterano" cliques and those active in the late 1970s there had been fourteen cliques in White Fence and seventeen in El Hoyo Maravilla. In the recent cliques, the gang structure was less clear-cut. This may be considered another stage in the development of these gangs for a variety of reasons.

First, members were beginning to "jump" from one clique to another. In some gangs studied elsewhere in the nation, members "graduate" from "junior" to "senior" cliques when they prove themselves (see Suttles, 1968; Hagedorn, 1988). This has not been the tradition in these East Los Angeles gangs. All of the earlier cliques were clearly separated by age. But in more recent cliques, there appears to be considerably more movement from clique to clique. This is not quite "graduation," yet it is not the firm segregation of the earlier cliques. This may well be related to the fact that men remain attached to the gangs longer, and the institution is really changing (see Chapter Seven).

Second, it is also related to changes in the prison culture. Thus, in recent years, men in prison may switch from one clique to another. Thus it happened that an imprisoned lone White Fence Spider switched for protection to the White Fence Termites (who had several members in prison at the time). By contrast, in earlier years, no such switching was necessary because members of all cliques of the same gang banded together no matter what the clique.

Finally, a possibly anomalous pattern was found in the White Fence gang: The territory claimed by the gang had expanded dramatically to incorporate at least four small neighboring gangs. By the late 1970s the territory was so large that the cliques were beginning to split a little bit. Closer neighbors tended to hang around as much with each other as with the larger clique.

There were fewer apparent changes in the girls' cliques. In El Hoyo they continued to show considerable autonomy. One of the Ganzas talked about how her clique got started and how it came to be affiliated with the male Ganzos clique:

It was in the summer of 1969. I was hanging around with a couple of girls but we were just starting out as teenagers. We were discussing about starting up a club. It was about 5 of us. I was going to Belvedere Junior High at that time, and all of a sudden I was meeting with a lot of the girls and it all fell into place. We went down to the park and we were just ditching down there. We were just hanging round. We were all about 15 or 16 years old and we were talking about making a club. "Let's name it '69ers' or something like that" because of the year.

Well I don't know how it happened but the men—the Ganzos— were down there. They were looking for girls to back them up and they would be called the Ganzas. So they seen us sitting there on a bench and they came over to us and asked us if we were interested in joining them. . . . So we went ahead and we told them that we would. They just told us, "OK, you just have to fight one another and that's how you get all of you in." So we said, "Oh man." We thought it was pretty silly. I guess we were all looking for a feeling of being wanted, so we went and did it. We were all fighting and what have you. Then they handed us a can of spray paint and some baggies and we were on our way!

True to the traditions of El Hoyo, though, the Ganzas dated not only the Ganzos, but also the male Locos clique, as did members of the female Locas clique, which was ostensibly connected to the Locos.

And true to the traditions in White Fence, each of the younger women's cliques in that neighborhood seem to have been attached to just one clique of the boys. Thus the Monstras started in 1970 with just three girls hanging around with the original Monstros. One girl left after a year and a half, because "the clique was a flop." A girl who persisted commented: "Well see, when the Monstras first started up we almost didn't keep going because we weren't getting enough girls, and [the boys, the Monstros] were telling us that we had to get more girls, pressuring us, so that's when we started getting more girls and making it bigger."

In the mid-1980s, there may have been a new phase of institutional change in the gangs. The traditional gangs were clearly labeled *cholos*.[2] But new groups of boys began to show up in the barrios that called themselves Stoners. Police believed that they were a total departure from the traditional Chicano gangs, and that they were involved in satanism. (The groups listened to heavy-metal music, and some of the lyrics of favorite rock groups involved references to the devil.) Actually, the police perception about satanism was incorrect, at least in the two neighborhoods we studied. The Stoners did represent a significant stylistic departure from the traditional cholo gang dress and taste in music, which had evolved slowly from the flamboyant pachuco style of the 1940s. Cholos wore neatly ironed chinos or jeans, along with loosely buttoned woolen Pendleton shirts and slicked-back hair; Stoners wore Led Zepplin T-shirts and long hair and athletic shoes. Cholos liked to listen to oldies—1950s music—and Stoners did not.

In El Hoyo Maravilla, the Stoners clique were clearly part of the barrio tradition, and were considered just the most recent of the gang's cliques. And in the mid-1980s a group of Stoners calling themselves The Hill began hanging around a street corner in White Fence, and "putting graffiti out." The hangout was directly across the street from a major rival of White Fence—Varrio Nuevo (VNE) (based in the Estrada Courts housing project). Varrio Nuevo also had a Stoner gang, and The Hill and the VNE Stoners fought bitterly. In addition, the White Fence Hill boys backed up the traditional White Fence cholo clique in fights, and the Stoners backed up the traditional VNE clique. When the mother of one boy was asked what was the difference between the Hill and a gang, she said, "They're not cholos. That's the only difference." By 1990, Stoners in both neighborhoods appear to had been integrated into the existing gang structure.

Gang Programs

Traces of public and private programs to affect Los Angeles gangs appeared as far back as the days of World War II. A basketball tournament was developed for the original White Fence gang and sponsored by the YMCA. This competition was one of the first signs of something important in public policy: Gangs in Los Angeles would never be allowed to evolve by themselves. A host of organizations would continually impinge on their lives. In fact, these programs are complicated enough to warrant a separate history. Here we can only sketch an outline.

The first serious efforts at gang programs in East Los Angeles came in the 1940s, as a response to the moral panic that developed with the Zoot-Suit Riots. They were both public and private, including programs by the Los Angeles County Probation Department (the Group Guidance Unit, established in 1944) and by the Community Chest (forerunner of the United Way). The White Fence gang was an early target of these programs and sent representatives to the Federation of Youth Clubs (Dwoskin, 1948). The services were intended for "hard-to-reach groups" and had the plain purpose of dissolving the gang. Family and neighborhood were both defined as "damaging" and "disorganizing" influences for the youngsters (Dieppa, 1973; Smith, 1964).[3]

Generally, the focus of gang work in the 1940s was on sports—boxing, a baseball club—and, later, dances. This was what some members recall as the "golden age of sports," when Chicano barrios were meeting each other in sports competitions that attracted large audiences. They were sponsored by local businessmen who bought jackets, trophies, and other legitimating symbols.

The earliest cliques in El Hoyo were served by gang workers from the Catholic Youth Organization (CYO) with close linkages to a nearby church. One man recalled a priest who was "sort of a gang worker. He taught us how to take care of our bodies, moral standards—what was bad and good. I thought of him as a very kind man, very thoughtful." Because El Hoyo Maravilla was located in the unincorporated portion of Los Angeles County, it was only a minor target of gang workers. Respondents generally regretted the absence of programs. Here is a Maravilla man: "I think it would have helped a lot of guys. I used to go down to Ford [nearby barrio with a settlement house] and work out with the guys and pull out my frustrations on the punching bag and go in the ring with my compadre and get my head knocked out. That's what they need out here, something—involvement, you know. Mostly cause if you stand on the corner, that's a frustration, just standing on the corner. No job, no nothing. And when asked, "Would it have been different if you had a club?" a Maravilla woman active during the same period answered, "It would have rules and regulations. This way it was just street rules. In the middle of the jungle."

By contrast to the neglect of the Maravilla gangs, during the 1940s and 1950s public and private gang workers were consistently assigned to the White Fence gang. The barrio was in the city of Los Angeles and, because it had a reputation for violence, it benefited from many of the city's responses to the periodic moral panics about gang violence. The first clique had two detached workers—one for the boys and one for the girls, and the YMCA provided a place to work out, to box, to shower, to train, and occasionally a place for runaway boys to stay.[4] The next cliques also had probation officers assigned to work with them, and in the late 1950s, as gang members recalled, a teen post was started in the White Fence neighborhood. For the next four cliques, the teen post was a fixture. The mother of a gang member began to work there and she became a surrogate mother to some of the boys. She was uniformly mentioned with respect. It is particularly noteworthy that this woman would typically telephone the boys' parents whenever there was trouble.

A very short-lived teen post was started in El Hoyo Maravilla in the mid-1960s, according to gang members. It, too, was directed by someone who had grown up in the barrio and was "helpful to our needs." The sponsor occasionally went to court with the boys as well as providing the usual pool tables, checkers, and activities that would "keep us off the street and keep us busy." One woman complained that the Maravilla teen post had no programs for girls.

The White Fence teen post was closed after a series of violent incidents. The most dramatic was an invasion by a rival gang, during which a boy was killed. No staff was present at the time, and the boy who was killed had been hidden in a closet because he was too stupefied by drugs to run away. The teen post was closed briefly, and reopened only to be bombed by another rival gang, whose members also shot into the place. The teen post stopped all gang work after these incidents. A younger woman commented: "If there hadn't been a teen post we would have been on the streets more. And when they took it off, we were back on the streets again. And I don't understand why they did it. You know, we could have been good kids. I was taking crocheting down there and they were taking cooking classes and stuff like that."

By the late 1970s, gang work was becoming something of an anachronism in East Los Angeles. One of the more influential works on gangs, Malcolm Klein's *Street Gangs and Street Workers* (1971) was based on studies of Los Angeles street gangs. Klein argued that gang workers enhance the attractiveness of gangs by focusing attention on the members. He recommended that traditional gang work be abandoned in favor of individualized treatment that focuses on dissolving gang attachments. In the hands of Los Angeles policymakers, however, this recommendation was taken as an injunction to end gang programs altogether. It was espoused with special enthusiasm by police and sheriffs, who were increasingly successful in persuading policymakers to substitute beefed-up police gang squads. One gang program after another was eliminated during this period.

Publicly and privately funded gang programs frequently hired paraprofessionals as outreach workers, and the vast majority were former gang members (Salcido, 1979) who prided themselves on their knowledge of the community and their ability to pull errant gang youth back in line. But there was also what might be called grass roots programming, as exemplified by the efforts of the Chicano movement in the 1960s. Community activists took the reduction of gang warfare as a serious goal (see Moore et al., 1978:41–44; Erlanger, 1979). Hundreds of murals appeared throughout the barrios, focusing on ethnic and militant themes, and many expressed the tragedy of deaths in gang warfare. The militant Chicano youth group, the Brown Berets, organized gang members. They established a coffee house for rap sessions and a newspaper (Fox, 1970).

In later years, spontaneous efforts to curb the killings were made by older gang members in a number of neighborhoods. One of our respondents, a man who had been active in the Chicano movement, developed a program in his own barrio—El Hoyo Maravilla:

> I implemented a program, for two years. It was funded, and it brought down crime in El Hoyo Mara, which was my target area. Brought it down 30 percent the first year and 56 percent the second year—drastically. Deaths were not even in the barrio. [The name of the program was?] MYSCOP. Maravilla Youth and Senior Citizens Organization. And what we did, we got the gang youth to work with the senior citizens, because 99 percent of the crime there was against the senior citizens. We got them to work on the community itself. If the gang thinks so much about the community, then let them praise it by bringing it up.

This man also began pressuring absentee landlords to clean up empty lots and dilapidated housing. Unfortunately, he could not obtain enough funding to continue the program. (see also Frias, 1982, for an innovative example that originated in the Arizona Maravilla barrio).

By the late 1980s, when we did our interviewing, apart from police activity, the only significant programs in East Los Angeles were specifically focused on the reduction of gang violence. In one such program sponsored by the California Youth Authority, gang members were hired to cool out potential gang fights in their own barrios. Another, funded by the city and county, had a similar goal (see Reinhold, 1988). Almost inevitably, despite formal limitations, these workers found themselves playing broader roles. From the perspective of most of our respondents, programs directed at normalizing gang members were of real use. They rarely transformed either the gang or any gang member, but they provided important links to conventionality—links that were missing for increasing proportions of the young gang members.

Understanding Changes in the Youth Gang

What happened to the gangs between the 1950s and the 1970s? What changes can we find in recruitment; sociability, especially the use of drugs and expressions of sexuality; violence; and linkages to conventional barrio life? And in what conceptual context do we understand this? In the next two chapters I describe the substance of these changes. In the remainder of this chapter I discuss various ways of understanding these changes.

Few researchers have considered how gangs change. Almost all examinations of gangs have been one-shot portraits, heavily focused on gangs as youth groups. Obviously, as quasi-institutions in their neighborhoods, these gangs evolve over time. But how do they evolve? It is important to separate out two phases of the gang: the adolescent phase and the adult phase. Although the two are of course linked, different processes of change may be working in the world of adolescents as compared with the world of adults.

"Normal Deviance": Are Gangs Outside the Normal Range of an Evolving Adolescent Subculture?

Community-oriented sociologists define gangs not in terms of delinquency, but rather in terms of group processes. Short, for example, defines "gang" as follows: "A group whose members meet together with some regularity, over time, on the basis of group-defined criteria of membership and group-determined organizational structure, usually with some sense of territoriality" (Short, 1990). Short goes on to comment that his definition "includes neither delinquent nor conventional behaviors, since these usually are what we wish to explain."

Like any good sociologist, Short emphasizes the need to understand variations in gang behavior. In his theory of "normal deviance," Fine (1987) permits us to put ganging into both a community and a developmental perspective. This perspective, in turn, allows us to look at change over time. Preadolescent and adolescent males tend to gang together, and Fine argues that two "imperatives of development"—sex and aggression—depend largely on what happens in the peer group (1987:104). Fine neglects a third "developmental imperative"—one that involves experimentation with alcohol and drugs. The use of drugs and alcohol in American adolescence centers on questions about self-control and identity (see Hawkins, Lishner, and Catalano, 1985), and management of such substances is also learned almost entirely in the peer group.[5]

Fine explains why youngsters acting out these developmental imperatives flirt with deviance, even in groups that are completely conventional. The group serves as the audience for acts that imitate older boys' sexuality, aggressiveness, and intoxication. It establishes its own norms for appropriate behavior in each of these realms. Thus a boy may "'go too far' or 'not far enough,' and both types of boys are disparaged (as 'rowdies' or 'faggots')" (1987:122). Thus the members define what is deviant or normal within each particular group.

However, they are convinced that adults will be horrified at their behavior. Even relatively innocent pranks must be kept secret. Thus secrecy and protection of prankster members become part of the group's culture. It is "normal deviance."

These are exactly the processes that go on within the gangs. The internal dynamics are the same: there is much display of "manly" sexuality and aggressiveness, much play with getting loaded on alcohol and drugs, much intragroup insults and jockeying for status. Each clique establishes its own norms for judging members' deviance. Traditionally, in the gangs, it was one-on-one fair fighting that established the status order within the gang, and a boy's reputation was established not only in fights between gangs, but also within the gang. Each clique also had a distinct culture based on its own short history, and a deep sense of secrecy and protectiveness of members from adults and outsiders in general. A sense of loyalty was a paramount value.

What does normal deviance theory suggest about change in gangs? Normal deviance theory permits us to look at the so-called deviance of the gangs as the normal play of adolescent males with universal developmental needs to experiment with sexuality, aggressiveness, and self-control within a peer group. It also conceptualizes peer groups as arrayed in any given community along a continuum. This continuum runs from what Fine calls "goody-goody" to "rowdy." Even though sociologists often treat gangs as if they were totally isolated delinquent phenomena, in fact gang members go to school, and their group is one of many in the school youth-culture setting.

This perspective on youth gangs—that they are special groups within which normal developmental needs are filled—may help to understand the changes within the gangs that I discuss in the next two chapters. It is an approach that has its limitations: Most notably, it does not help much to understand the girl gangs. Campbell (1984) argues that gang girls used to be portrayed solely as sex objects, and their gangs solely as female auxiliaries, but it is clear that such a portrayal does not apply to the gangs we study. Thus the general notion that gang girls have moved away from such "traditional roles" in recent years must also be taken with a grain of salt. Perhaps both views represent stereotypes: Thus one writer in the 1970s commented that black gang girls go through essentially the same processes as boys in using the gang to establish identity, and this may well be valid for Chicanas as well (Brown, 1977, cited in Fishman, 1988).

The point is that the youth-culture continuum from goody-goody to rowdy shifts over time. The goody-goodiest group in the community today is considerably more active sexually, for example, than in the past. And the rowdiest group—the gang—is likely to slip much further in the direction of real deviance. Over the past generation American adolescents in general began to act out more. The gang can be expected to be more deviant as the adolescent subculture in general becomes more deviant. This is one significant source of change: The adolescent gang "leads" in ordinary adolescent trends, especially those involving peer-regulated developmental imperatives.

How Do Gangs Evolve?

Gang deviance is usually seen as anything but normal, and there are two significant theoretical scenarios about how the deviance of gangs may evolve. They are absolutely opposed to each other. The first may be called resistance theory, and the second the illicit opportunity scenario. Both deal with what happens to gang members as they mature—or fail to mature—out of adolescent gang concerns.

Resistance Theory.   The first idea is that gangs are potentially revolutionary organizations of youth that give voice to the frustrations of oppressed minorities. This has been applied particularly to Chicano gangs (Frias, 1982; Mirande, 1987). There is no doubt that in the 1960s militant youth organizations such as the Chicano Brown Berets and the Puerto Rican Young Lords drew on gangs for the members (see Erlanger, 1979). Militant rhetoric was also essential to the self-help movement of Chicano gang members in prison (see Moore et al., 1978).

While this view of the possible evolution of gangs may have dimmed during the distinctly nonrevolutionary 1970s and 1980s, it retains its adherents among the more romantic observers. A more sophisticated and plausible variation of gangs as resistance groups is propounded by several English writers, but, ironically, the end result is that the gangs do *not* change, nor does their resistance have much effect on their life circumstances. This idea is that the gangs, like other working-class youth groups, are "oppositional" because they do and say things that challenge and flout conventional authority. They resist definitions that come from above, conducting a "guerilla warfare" against the alien bourgeois culture of existing institutions—a resistance movement (Corrigan, 1979).

But, as Willis (1981) points out, this very culture of defiance at best dooms the boys to jobs just like those their fathers hold, and transfers the defiant and subversive attitude from school to workplace. And, in counterpart, similar mechanisms may prepare adolescent female "resistors" for a lifetime of subordination as wives (Lees, 1986). In effect, the male peer group becomes good socialization for lower-level working jobs.

Resistance theory thus winds up with a paradoxical view of gangs as potentially revolutionary organizations. It sees the functions of adolescent group defiance (or resistance) as serving to keep working-class kids in the working class. Defiance and resistance are, in effect, an energetic spinning of the wheels: but not revolutionary.

The Illicit Opportunity Scenario.   The opposing view is that gangs evolve into criminal organizations, in which the adolescent cohorts serve as recruiting and training grounds for adult criminal enterprises. This is the view that emerges from Cloward and Ohlin's classic look (1960) at "criminal" as contrasted with "violent" or "retreatist" gangs (see also Shaw and McKay, 1943). They distinguished three types of gangs—criminal, violent, and retreatist. Each is to be found in a special kind of lower-class community. All three types of gang arise from disparities between aspirations of young persons and the opportunities they could find in poor communities. This is generally the view that is implicit in much traditional law enforcement imagery of the gangs, especially as it is amplified in the media (see Morgenthau et al., 1988).[6]

Several recent studies of gangs in the Midwest also implicitly adopt this view. A historical study of Chicago gangs sees the increased involvement of black gangs in drug trafficking as a response to continued racism and to economic problems within the community (Perkins, 1987). A study of a Puerto Rican gang, also in Chicago, sees the gang as an ethnic enterprise, shifting its activities quite consciously toward street dealing in a community where good jobs have become increasingly hard to find (Padilla, 1990).

This scenario is essentially in line with Wilson's work on the devastating effects of economic restructuring. Good factory jobs have disappeared and been replaced by poor-paying service jobs. Welfare, bartering, informal economic arrangements, and illegal economies become substitutes—simply because people must find a way to live. Young people growing up in such communities have little good to anticipate. In this changing environment, youth groups adapt by entering what Padilla calls "ethnic enterprises"—illicit income-generating activities. Both Padilla and Philippe Bourgois (who studies Puerto Rican life in New York) note that these young people also consciously regard their illicit activities as resistance to the humiliation and demeaning experiences they face in the licit job market.

The problems generated by economic restructuring in the inner city are increasingly conspicuous. Researchers on inner-city gangs almost by necessity are examining community and cultural variations. The basic theme of these researchers—opportunity structures—may be the same as Cloward and Ohlin's (1960), but the theme is specified in different ways by various researchers. Sullivan (1989) shows how much variation there is from one neighborhood to another in youth group response to economic change.

How Useful Are These Perspectives in White Fence and El Hoyo Maravilla?

Between the 1950s and 1970s the gangs of East Los Angeles did change. But clearly, they did not become criminal organizations. Nor

did the ideology of Chicanismo and the revolutionary oppositional elements ever develop. Police label gang activities as criminal and radicals
label them revolutionary, and both labels capture some elements of the
complex reality. But neither captures the essence of the gang, and the
picture of change that emerges fits only partially into the three theoretical
frameworks just described.

In Chapter Two I discussed the disappearance of good manufacturing jobs in East Los Angeles, and their replacement by low-wage, unsheltered work—with a lot of competition from exploitable immigrants.
These changes are typical of the national economic restructuring during the period. They provide the context within which these rowdiest
of adolescent groups became increasingly rowdier—still in the van of
long-term shifts in American youth culture.

chapter four

Changes in the Gangs

These two gangs had been active for more than forty-five years when we did our study. Over those years, they became quasi-institutionalized. Each clique is part of a continuing institution. In this chapter I discuss changes in recruitment and initiation patterns, changes in patterns of sociability and drug use, changes in gender-related attitudes, and changes in violence. These last three concerns touch on drugs, sexuality and violence, and reflect our interest in the gang as a socializing institution in which adolescent identity issues get acted out. They also reflect a more general question about gangs: Have they become more—or less—deviant?

Gangs and the Evolution of Deviance

The first answer to the question of deviance is that the gang has an inherent tendency toward an increase in deviance. Each clique forms while its predecessor is active and visible on the streets. It forms, generally, with the sense that it can match or outdo its predecessor. The norms of conduct and the myths and legends of its predecessor clique also become part of the gang's general culture (see Cohen, 1955). They may be learned from relatives who were in the older cliques and from stories passed on by older clique members in youth detention facilities and in adult facilities, where older members of the gang may act as a repository of gang lore.

Stories about the gang in jail become part of the gang's general mythic heritage. Gang members who go to prison tend to regress into a strong gang orientation. Gangs have long been a major influence in California prisons, and for a new inmate his gang provides companionship, protection, and access to benefits (see Moore et al., 1978). When they return from prison often they are unable to find work, and are more than willing to share their own "glory days" (with suitable exaggeration) with the younger kids who hang around the park. Thus the clique structure of the gang means that in addition to each clique's own mini-culture, the clique has the general culture of the gang—both in the streets and in the prisons—to draw upon for myths and legends of prowess. These legends invariably represent far more extreme behavior than displayed by most members of the clique itself. On top of all this, most cliques want to outdo their predecessors in acts of derring-do, which may involve violence, or drug use, or sexual activity. This also adds to the potential for a growth in deviance over time.

A second answer to the question of deviance is that the gangs were never permitted to evolve independently. The gangs have been subject to organized efforts at control. The most persistent pressures come from the police, often with overheated attention from the mass media. And, as I discussed in Chapter Three, both of our gang neighborhoods have seen sporadic efforts at gang programming, some begun as far back as the 1940s. Generally these programs did not last more than a few years.

There is considerable controversy about gang programs. Some argue that they simply enhance the attractiveness of the gang by enlarging its resources (Klein, 1971). Others argue that programs do reduce the inherent tendency to increased deviance by reducing the gang's isolation from conventional socializing influences. In view of the sporadic nature of gang programming, such controversies may be meaningless, because the evidence is so erratic.

Similar arguments are made about enhanced criminal-justice system activities. Some argue that heavy-handed police and court actions fail to control gang activity and may in fact enhance it by increasing members' resentment and generating further disaffection and isolation (Hagedorn, 1988). Others take police activity at face value, as controlling the deviance.

Controversies about the effectiveness of programs and of police activities tend to neglect the local community. In fact, the more respectable members of local communities have often become significant forces in helping label the gang as deviant and further isolating it. Other segments, equally respectable, continue to try to integrate gang members into conventional community life (see Moore, 1985).

Taking the local community, gang programming, and police all into account it is difficult to draw a balance. It seems clear that the gangs as quasi-institutions in these communities became comparatively autonomous, with their own norms, myths, and legend constantly amplified. A newly formed gang has few traditions and only a brief history. Old, established gangs claim stronger traditions and, perhaps, deeper loyalties. For a member of a long-established gang to "let down the flag" carries a sense of violating long-standing traditions. Thus, in sum, we suggest that membership in these older established gangs with long-standing reputations may encourage deviance simply because they compete more effectively with other agencies of socialization—especially schools and family.

Joining the Gang

Changes in recruitment patterns are often a good way to look at institutional changes. We know for certain that the cliques of the 1950s recruited younger members in a narrow age span but that cliques of the 1970s recruited older members across a broader age span. Men in the cliques active in the 1950s joined at significantly earlier ages—a median of age 13 as compared to age 14 for the more recent cliques. In those earlier cliques almost no boy joined the gang over the age of 15, but in the recent cliques, almost a third of the men joined at ages 16 or older. Both older and younger women joined at a median of 13.5 years. In the newer cliques 20 percent of the women joined at ages 16 or older.

Thus the earlier cliques recruited almost exclusively during early adolescence, while the more recent cliques continued to recruit into late adolescence. This is related to changes in maturing out of the gang. In the more recent cliques, higher proportions continued to hang around on the streets—and they continued to recruit new members of their own age—that is, the late teens. In earlier cliques, by late adolescence the only men still identified with the gang were those who had become involved in the heroin life-style—and they avoided the younger kids entirely.

How did members come to join? Among the boys, there were many avenues to membership, and older cliques were not notably different from younger ones. Almost all of the men (89 percent) claimed to have lived in the gang's territory while they were growing up, and some drifted into membership through neighborhood and school friends. Two older men were asked, "Why did you join the gang?" One, from El Hoyo Maravilla, answered, "I have no idea. I don't. I just fell into it. . . . I just happened to live there in the environment. . . . Just from going to school, and knowing the guys, and living there, and talking with the guys every day in school. Of course all this started when I started going to Belvedere Junior High School at the age of 13. This is when I started meeting different guys from around, and I just happened to hang around with them." The other answered, "I guess by association, you know. I was in elementary school and the members of the White Fence gang that was in the school that they went to and we met there. [?] I would say like raised into the gang. In other words you know we went to school together, and we played together and you know just became probably like being raised into the gang." Approximately 10 percent of the boys were actively recruited, even if they lived outside the neighborhood, usually because they were potentially good fighters: "Well, I had been living two years on 4th and Bernal [in the White Fence neighborhood], and I was hanging around on Bernal, and these guys seen me, and I was tall, so they wanted me to join the gang." A significant fraction were strongly attracted to the gang: "Because [El Hoyo Maravilla] had a lot of fame: a lot of people knew about it, so I wanted to belong." Sometimes a strong gang offered protection, as for this younger woman: "Just like from school there was another gang and they said that if I didn't get into their gang they were gonna jump me and all that. But then my sister was from White Fence and the girls from White Fence said 'Just join us and nothing's gonna happen.'" In many cases, motives were obviously mixed, as with this younger Maravilla man: "I lived there. I grew up there. It was just natural. It's the most natural thing to be from a gang. I always wanted to be because of the reputation El Hoyo had. They had the biggest as I grew up."

Even though most of the women (65 percent) also claimed to live in the gang neighborhood during their early teens, the pattern of being "raised into the gang" because of living in the neighborhood was less common among the girls. They were more likely to join through relatives and close friendships, including, occasionally, boyfriends. Women were also more likely to mention problems at home when they talked about joining the gang. Two older women's experiences differed. One recounted, "There was a period of years that my mother was dying, and the family got real loose. We got real loose since she wasn't in the home. She was in the hospital. I started going down to the Hole, El Hoyo." And the other remembered, "When I first backed up White Fence I was about 11. I mean anybody put down my barrio I stuck up for it, you know. Whether I was with other gang members or not, you know. I mean nobody put down White Fence in my presence, you know, cause I say, 'Hey, you don't talk that way about my barrio, you know. This is where I live, you know.'" One of two younger women said, "I just, ah—I met [my boyfriend from White Fence] and just started hanging around there. Then the girls talked me into getting in, and I got in." The other commented, "I was raised into—well, not raised, but umm it's because I used to help them [White Fence] so much they considered me one of them, because I was always there, helping out in their fights. I lived there. That's how I got into it."

It is one of the strongest police and newspaper myths about these gangs that membership is "inherited," that is, passed on from father to son. But such cases are rare among either men or women. It is true that about half of the gang members had some relative in some gang (44 percent of the men and 59 percent of the women). It is true that young members were significantly more likely than older ones to have a relative. It is true that a fraction (less than 20 percent) of the gang members came from what seem to be "gang families"—with three or more relatives in a gang and steeped in gang traditions. But there were very few such families in either neighborhood. Rather than "inheritance" being the norm, most relatives were brothers and cousins and uncles rather than parents (see Vigil, 1988b).[1]

No matter what particular social network led the member to the gang, one thing is clear: the gangs' initiation procedures became far more ritualized. By the time the younger cliques were active, most of the boys and girls were "jumped" into the gang, in an initiation rite in which the recruit is tested for his/her ability to stand up in a fight. Almost none of the members of older cliques went through this ordeal. There was no initiation ritual. The gang asked prospects to join and that was it.

In sum, gangs of the 1970s were less clearly adolescent groups than the gangs of the 1950s. While there were still many social routes to enter the gang, the younger cliques contained more men and women with relatives who had been gang members. And, finally, the gangs had acquired the accoutrements of ritualized initiations.

Going Down to the Barrio, Partying, and Getting Loaded

Gang members spend most of their time together just "hanging around" at some special spot in the neighborhood or in smaller friendship cliques just as any group of high-school friends in any city would tend to meet regularly in the same place with the same friends. Few of the men had good friends outside the gang. (This was also true for almost all of the younger women, but only a quarter of the older women had nongang friends.) As one man reminisced about a White Fence hangout, "It just—you know, we went to the Lane [a dead-end street] and just hung around there. It's like a lot of grass, palm trees. We used to sit around and just drink and listen to the radio and talk with the girls and stuff like that." (In fact, the Lane was a rather barren, graffiti-smeared, but isolated, part of the neighborhood.) Occasionally the favorite hangout was an undeveloped overgrown hilly spot in the neighborhood, or the front porch or backyard of a permissive parent, or (as in El Hoyo Maravilla in the 1970s) a corner of a neighborhood park. Gang members could not leave their neighborhood without running into fights with rival gangs, and for many, hanging around became the essence of gang sociability—what they meant by "partying."

But "partying" for these gang members, as for many American adolescents, has also been associated with getting high. We asked, "What kind of partying were you doing then?" Males were most likely to respond with some mention of drinking or getting high, although women (especially the older ones) also mentioned dancing as a major definition of "partying." One younger White Fence woman discussed partying: "It was just like having fun, just sitting around, hearing oldies, dancing, drinking." Another commented, "That's when Pumkin had the garage in the back. We would go there and we'd be partying back there. We'd have dances. [You mean where they live right now still?] Yeah, in the back. I remember because we used to get so fucked up, and it was all dirt. Somebody would fall, and we used to have to pick them up."

Most commonly, "getting high" meant alcohol and marijuana to both older and younger cliques, with PCP and barbiturates common among the younger groups as well. (See Long, 1990, for details about drug use in these cliques.) Here similar sociability patterns are reported in both generations, with enhanced drug use in the younger generation (perhaps reflecting greater affluence): According to an older Maravilla man, partying "was like getting together, getting some money—see how much money we could raise to get a bottle of wine. [OK, drinking. Was there any smoking weed, or anything like that?] Occasionally, yes. [OK. Did you have any house parties?] Not at *my* house, but at other houses, yes. [What kinds of drugs were people into using then?] Only pot. [Any pills?] No." A younger White Fence man said that partying was "hanging around with the crowd, right there in the neighborhood, go to dances right there in the neighborhood. [What kind of drugs were people in the clique into using then?] Heroin, angel dust, marijuana, reds, sniffing glue."

Especially in the younger cliques, drugs for parties were usually bought from one of the boys in the clique or from some member of an older clique. According to several informants, the Hoyo Maravilla neighborhood had no dealers at all during the 1930s and early 1940s, not even dealers in marijuana. The earlier gang members bought marijuana from dealers in another gang (the First and Evergreen gang).[2] Here are reminiscences from a (probably boastful) older and a younger man about the sources of drugs used at parties:

[What kind of partying did you mostly do in your clique?] Well I have to, I have to say, that we used to use a whole lot of yellow jackets and weed. Heavy drugs came in later on. . . . [About how many of the kids that you knew from the clique were dealing?] Well, I was dealing so that's one. Besides me, ah, then I used to give some of the pills to other guys from my clique to deal. I would say about that I knew for a fact, you know, ah, about 3 guys. [OK, what were they dealing mostly?] Yellow jackets. [How did you guys get the drugs when you were partying?] I used to do all the burglaries, down the hospitals. I used to break in, and get the big jars, which was about, I don't know how many pills they contained, but they sure had a bunch of them. Over a thousand pills a jar.

[What kind of partying did you mostly do in your clique?] Mostly getting loaded with girls, and going to parties, house parties. [What kind of drugs were people in the cliques into using then?] Mostly marijuana, and barbiturates, reds, downers. [About how many of the kids from the clique did you know were dealing?] Really not too many, maybe a little weed here and there, but nobody was into heavy

52 chapter four

drugs. [Would you say an approximate actual number?] Maybe like
ten of them. [What were they dealing mostly?] Marijuana, weed.
[How did you get the drugs when you were partying?] From older
people, older homeboys. Most of the time we bought them. Unless
from some older brother, or good friends.

Even though drugs were almost universal—especially with the
younger cliques—respondents generally reported that the few members
who never used drugs at parties were accepted and not pressured to
use drugs. This tolerance was especially notable in the older cliques, but
even in the younger cliques only 12 percent of the men and 15 percent of
the women reported that they pressured abstainers. Thus even though
these adolescents experimented widely with drugs, individual variations
in taste were accepted within this friendship peer group.

Very few used heavy drugs during gang partying. Heroin was the
most serious drug at the time in these neighborhoods: cocaine did not
appear as a significant drug until the late 1980s. (Even then, cocaine did
not displace heroin, and despite its epidemic status on the other side of
town, crack cocaine made little headway among these gang members.)
However, only a few men (13 percent of the sample) and fewer women
(6 percent) reported that they used heroin in their early teens. Most
began in their later teens, when more than half of the men and a quarter
of the women used heroin. The heroin users tended to withdraw into
their own subcliques, largely because their heroin-centered life-styles
engulfed them. Getting heroin involves a constant hustle: There is no
time for anything else. "They phased off.[3] [?] Well once you start taking
heroin, it cuts you down; you're not yourself, and you don't have the
strength you used to have, you know what I mean, because it drains you.
[Where would they go off on their own?] Who knows where they go, you
know, just to support their habits. [OK, so they didn't have that much
time for the gang any more; they had to worry about—]—the next fix,
you know."

In the older cliques, when heroin was first introduced, the nonusing
gang members tended to reject the users. Users attracted police attention, and they were also likely to leech off their fellow gang members:
"They mostly went on their own. [?] Because we used to tell them 'Don't
hang around with us,' you know. But in case there was something [fight],
they'd back us up. At that time we didn't care for it. The guys that were

using, they thought they knew it all, too. They'd say [about us] 'These guys are squares.' "

In sum, hanging around and partying were and remain the major activity of these gangs, with drugs as a continuous part of the scene: The gang *is* after all, the rowdiest crowd around. However, heroin is not generally a party drug, and heroin users tended—especially in the past—to withdraw into their own subcliques.

Girls in the Gang: Gender-Related Perceptions

These were male-oriented groups, and there was considerable disagreement about the role of girls in the gang. We asked rather pointed questions to probe into this general area: "In the gang, some of the girls said that the guys just treat them like possessions. How true do you think that was for your clique?" Most of the women—almost two-thirds, older and younger—vehemently denied the truth of such assertions. A White Fence woman said, "No, I think my homeboys treated us good, the way we should be treated. Every individual—they treated me like Chena; they treated Tinker like Tinker. Maybe they got out of hand with some of the other ones, but in my day they treated us the way we should be treated, with respect." Often the women disagreed with the statement because they had rejected any attempts to dominate them. An older Maravilla woman commented, "We used to boss the guys!" And a younger White Fence woman said, "We did what we wanted. We didn't let the guys tell us what to do. Sometimes they would tell us, 'No, you can't go with the guys,' but we wouldn't listen to them, you know."

More of the men—and especially the younger men—agreed that the boys treated the girls like possessions (41 percent of the older men and 56 percent of the younger men, reflecting an increase.) Among those who denied such sexism, the keynote was that the gang was like a family. A younger man said: "We treated them like our family. We respected them." An older Maravilla man made the same kind of argument, and in an idealistic evocation of the golden age of the past, implied that things had changed since his time: "That was very untrue, because we didn't have girl gang members back then. They were all our sisters, and we all respected them, so it was a lot different than what's happening now."

But among the men who agreed with the statement there were three basic themes. All reflected male adolescent experimentation with masculinity. The first theme rejected girls as gang members, arguing that the gang is a male preserve, and any girl who joins is worthless and deserves whatever happens to her. Here is a man from one of the younger White Fence cliques:

> [Why do you say that the boys treated the girls like possessions?] Because they belong to a gang and any other guys they figure that if a girl is in the gang a girl would know better. I mean a girl shouldn't belong in no gang, because that's only for the guys. . . . They treat the girls right, but I don't think the motive was for a girl being in a gang. [?] They treat the girl right, but some guys don't see it that way, they see it different. They say, you know, they might get high and they start treating them bad and rough when they get high, like a regular guy. Because they know she shouldn't belong in the neighborhood out in the streets; she should be home with her mother or taking care of her little sister or brother, whatever, doing something else. Doing some chores.

The second theme emphasized the legitimacy of male dominance over women. An older man commented, "Well, I could answer in this way. When you're young you want to be on top. You don't want no girls telling you what to do. You want to be the man. [?] It used to happen to me all the time. I had a girlfriend named Pepe. She was involved with the gang. I used to run her home all the time." And a younger man said, "It's true. [?] Well, we'd just tell them, 'You're mine. You ain't going anywhere. Stay. I'm going. You're not.' You know, like we were overpowering them, I don't know."

The third theme, particularly articulated by younger men, emphasized sexuality, again reminiscent of Fine's (1987) "developmental imperatives." Sometimes the sexuality was rationalized as serving the higher needs of gang warriors: "Yes, at the time yes. I would say 90 percent was treated like a piece of ass. Whether it be a homegirl or any other girl. [?] Usually we [Hoyo Maravilla] just used them as sexual need things, and companions. We needed companions in sex. But at that time everybody thought [mainly] about the neighborhood and keeping the neighborhood image up."

But others were just interested in sex. Members in the more recent cliques did in fact become sexually active at earlier ages than members of the earlier cliques. The median age for boys' first sexual experience was

15.2 years in the earlier cliques, and 14.5 years in the recent cliques. The median age for girls' first sexual experience was 17.2 years in the earlier cliques and 16.0 in the more recent cliques.[4] Some of the boys were *only* interested in the gang girls as sex objects:

> Ah, it's just there, you know what I mean. The—you know, when you want a *chapete* (fuck) it was there, you know what I mean. [?] The guys treated them like shit, you know what I mean. And then when they wanted something you know, get it—wham bam. [Just use them for sex?] Yeah. Sex. Just to have a partner for the time, you know. They were just there, you know, we used to get them in, throw a *linea*, (lining up to have sex with a girl), you know what I mean.

It is important to realize that the full range of attitudes coexisted within almost every clique—earlier as well as more recent. Campbell (1984) argues that girl gangs have outgrown their sexist image, but we found no indication of change in the quality of sexism between older and younger cliques. In addition, it should be understood that many of these sentiments involve a good deal of projection: The brutal sex-object portrayal may be just as much of an exaggeration as the soft chivalrous attitude.

Certainly, women recalled the more sexually aggressive members with no affection. Many of the women in the gang were tough-minded, and effectively warded off boys' claims:

> Not *me*, they didn't treat *me* like that. They think we're possessions, but we're not. [?] Ah, they think that because we're from White Fence they can be with us, kiss us and stuff, but nah, I tell them, "Get away from me. Who do you think you are? Just because I'm a homegirl you think you can kiss me. I say get away from me." You know. No way. I pick my own boyfriends. I'll be with anybody I want to be with. You don't tell *me* who to be with.

By contrast, an older Maravilla woman left the gang because of an assault: "I remember one guy that was from the clique. He wanted to put a knife on me because he wanted to force me to be his old lady. I remember that guy. I'll never forget that guy. Since then I never wanted to be in the gang. He even put his sister to try and hold me, that cabrón!"

A gang girl who is raped by a homeboy is in a particularly bad position. If she complains, she is a "rat" (a police informant). The entire gang—girls included—go all out to protect their homeboy. One Maravilla woman commented that it was particularly important for the gang girls to go to court to back up their homeboys, because it helps the defense lawyer make the rape victim "look like a tramp." Rather wryly, she added "the girls don't get much credit for it."

Male possessiveness within the gangs is more than an attitude and can be manifested in very punitive reactions to girls who defy the norms. There are many stories about how gang girls manipulate their homeboys' possessiveness to incite gang fights. Most boys (74 percent) and girls (67 percent) dated partners from different gangs, as well. Often such dating meant risking a gang fight, since the dates were from rival gangs. "Those were dangerous territories," as one Maravilla man said. And, especially in the more recent cliques, there was just as much likelihood of violence from members of their own gang. Thus 83 percent of the women—old and young—reported that their gang homeboys were angry at such "disloyalty." An older Maravilla woman remembered: "I went out with guys from Diamond, from Dogtown, and I had a boyfriend in Mateo. [?] Well that one time they [the homeboys] found out about it, they didn't like it. They were waiting under the tree in the school and they threw cans at the guy that took me out. They broke the windows in his car, and they even threw trash cans at him." Sometimes cross-gang dating resulted in rape. In one case, two Hoyo Maravilla girls were picked up by boys from a rival gang (White Fence) and raped. When one of them was asked if her homeboys were upset about the rape, she said she didn't dare tell them about it: "Man, if they would even know that we were out doing that shit they would call us all kinds of names, and 'That's what you get for going with other guys from another neighborhood,' and stuff like that. Really!"

In the older cliques, boys reported that their homegirls generally accepted their dating girls from outside the clique, but 64 percent of the younger men reported that their homegirls reacted negatively. Such reactions—from homeboys as well as homegirls—were sometimes the sources of gang fights. "Sometimes they [the Maravilla homegirls] were jealous, but most of the time they usually ended up with guys from other neighborhoods, so there was really nothing they could say, usually. Unless you were with a homegirl and then left her for another girl from another neighborhood. That's what usually would start a war. Besides many wars started with other neighborhoods because of a love affair."

"If one of the guys is going out with a girl from the neighborhood and she drops him, and usually the guys are not going to accept being dropped. If she starts going out with a guy from another neighborhood, that's when problems start. She's still his, but she's saying, 'No, I'm not. I'm going my way.' That guy will go and start a hassle with *that* guy and there'll be a gang fight behind it."

Thus, as far as intergang dating is concerned, the changes seem to have enhanced gang loyalties to the point of increasing the risk of intergang violence, but it is also true that sometimes women negotiate with their homeboys about dating boys from other neighborhoods:

> Like when I was with a guy from Eastside Los [gang], that was terrible. They wanted to kick my butt and everything, you know, they just couldn't accept it. . . . And I said, "Hey, homes, you just have to accept it. I'm growing up, and I met this dude and I like him. He's treating me right and I want to be with him." . . . Eventually— it took time—but they did accept my old man. . . . It took a lot a lot of talking and a lot a lot a lot of talking to my homeboys. . . . It was because [her first boyfriend] he was from White Fence, so they thought that's the way it should have been, all along the line, all the way till death do us part. But you know it didn't work out that way.

In sum, there was not much difference between older and more recent cliques in the quality of mutual perceptions between boys and girls in the gang, even though men from the 1970s cliques were more likely to recognize that their attitudes were sexist. (This may be simply a generational phenomenon: Younger people in American society are generally more likely to be sensitive to sexism.) In any event, the double standard in these gangs was very strong, and while some girls flourished under it, for others it was a challenge.

But it is with aggression that the changes between the 1950s and 1970s become most evident.

Gang Violence and Gang Values

Until the early 1980s, these two gangs, along with other Chicano gangs in Los Angeles, were involved in serious and lethal gang warfare. Between 1970 and 1979 gang killings accounted for 16 percent of all Hispanic homicides in Los Angeles, but no more than 7 percent of homicides in other ethnic groups (Loya et al., 1986).[5]

There are many reasons for gang fights: invasion of territory, rivalry over dating, fights in conjunction with sports events, and personal matters in which the gang is brought in to back up an individual. But even during the most violent epoch, there was considerable variation in the levels of lethal violence from one clique to another of the gangs we study, and even within the same gang (see Moore, 1988). Measuring these changes poses some special problems.

Ideally, perhaps, the best measure of violence would be the number of deaths and hospitalizations inflicted by and suffered by any given clique over its lifetime. Our own measure falls short of this ideal. We have information only about the deaths suffered by the clique in gang fights. And even here members of the same clique reported different numbers. Only in one clique did all respondents agree: This was the only clique in which there were no killings at all.

Why is there so little firm agreement on such a traumatic event? The respondents had just refreshed their memories by checking over a roster of clique members. Therefore, the most obvious explanation—that memory is unreliable—is somewhat less convincing.

There are at least four other reasons for differences in reporting—and all cast some light on the nature of gang fighting. The most common is that a killing occurred just before the respondent joined the clique or just after he left. A second and related consideration is the size and duration of the clique. Some cliques were very small and lasted only a short time and their members agreed about the number of killings. Others were larger. One of our cliques was exceptionally large (five times the average size of other cliques) and was spread over a large territory. It lasted an unusually long time, continually recruiting. Thus, the clique encompassed a diverse group of men of very different ages. The size, duration, and territorial spread of a clique thus affect the experience of a gang member with a death. Third, a few respondents seemed to interpret the questions in terms of criminal activity, and answered "no" just as promptly and mendaciously as they answered "no" when asked how many were dealing drugs.

Finally, in some cases the association of a death with a gang activity was a matter of definition. Thus in one White Fence clique, there were no deaths during the clique's own fights, but one member was killed when

he went to the aid of the next youngest clique in one of their fights with
a traditional gang rival. Almost all of the respondents from this clique
claimed that one man had been killed, but two claimed that none had
died. And strictly speaking, there were no deaths during the course of
this clique's fighting history. One respondent expressed this ambiguity:

> [How many deaths were there to members of the clique during the
> peak activity?] During peak activities, I don't think there was none.
> Like not during that time, not injuries or nothing like that, death—
> but now I'm remembering that, you know, James—I think he died of
> an overdose or something? [No, they—] He was shot! [They shot
> him.] Shot, shot. But that was after, so, you know, we're talking
> about that period when they were in gang activities? I would say
> none. I would say none. [The fight in question occurred after the
> respondent—a White Fence Veterano—had left the gang and gotten
> married.]

There was considerable variation in the number of deaths in the eight
cliques: The range was from zero to a high of three. How can we account
for this variation? Here again we must examine the gang as an institution, with important continuities and evolution both in "reputation" and
in values.

The first thing that leaps immediately to view is that the cliques active
in the 1970s had more deaths than those active in the 1950s.[6] There are
at least two immediate explanations for this increase: One has to do with
the use of weapons and one is internal to the gang.

The most common explanation offered by our respondents for increased violence concerned weapons. Not only were more "real" guns
available in the 1970s compared with the homemade zip guns of 1950s
but guns were used for hurting people—aiming at the body, rather than
just scaring them by shooting in the air or at legs. An older White Fence
woman commented wryly: "You know it's easier for kids to get ahold of
guns and other weapons to fight with. Pulling the trigger now is called
gang fighting." A younger White Fence man acknowledged: "I think it
was easier for us to use a gun. . . . A lot of us are more apt to use a
piece." And, in fact, when asked about weapons that were used, younger
cliques—both male and female—were more likely to mention guns and
older ones to mention fistfights.[7]

Older members were also disturbed by the impersonality with which guns were used. For example, "drive-by shootings" were initiated in the 1970s. This new practice meant that gang members drove through a rival gang neighborhood, shooting into a target house or a corner gathering of teenagers. Drive-by shootings violated existing gang norms because they wounded and killed innocent bystanders—nongang youth, children, and old people.[8] Older members found this aggression against "noncombatants" particularly disturbing, along with what they saw as the virtual disappearance of "fair fights":

> There were some weapons used during my time, but not like now, in comparison to when I was growing up [in El Hoyo Maravilla]. It was mostly fighting—fair fights. Square off with a guy. [Fistfights?] Fistfights. If you lost, you just shook hands and that was it. [No weapons at all?] No, I wouldn't say no weapons at all. There were some weapons. Some knives, a few guns. But there was hardly any weapons showing when we used to fight.

"Fair fights" were sometimes as elaborately arranged as nineteenth-century duels: "He had a thing: he wanted to fight with me. He was with another guy, and I got a guy from First and Indiana [gang] to come and stand by and watch that other guy. I called him and told him, 'Hey look, I'm going to have it out with this asshole, but I don't want that other sucker jumping me.'" The demise of the fair fight and the rise in the impersonal use of weapons are related, according to older men. The fair fight established a pecking order, both within the gang and between gangs, and did so in a highly personal fashion that tested the mettle of the fighters in a way that guns cannot do.

Younger members often want to match or outdo the reputation of their predecessors. Respondents from the more violent cliques were significantly more likely to believe that their clique was more violent than its immediate predecessor.[9] Here is a member of the second girls' clique in White Fence responding to the question, "How did your clique compare to the one ahead of it in fighting: Was it more or less violent?"

> Ah, we couldn't beat the Honeydrippers [name of first girls' clique]. We weren't nothing in comparison to them as far as blows are concerned. We were trying to follow in their footsteps but we couldn't compare. [And how about the next youngest clique: How did your clique compare?] Well the little ones were just about as bad as we

were. I guess they were trying to follow in our footsteps and we were trying to follow in the other one's footsteps you see, but we couldn't compare to the Honeydrippers.

What else accounts for variations in the level of violence from clique to clique and escalation over time? Much has been made of the fact that Chicano gangs have had a more or less consistent subculture, and that some features of this gang subculture call for exaggeratedly "masculine behavior"—especially when it comes to aggressiveness. It is easy to label this subculture simply as macho, but machismo refers to control just as much as it does to aggressiveness. In fact, it is important to recognize that the most frequently expressed gang norm about fighting is that of control—both group control and individual control: "We [El Hoyo Maravilla] were not a gang that was looking for trouble. We would fight if somebody would pick on us, and we would fight to the end, but we wouldn't go around looking for a fight." Stoic endurance was the quality to be admired:

Well a lot of guys used to get stabbed. A lot of them weren't reported [back to the gang] you know. Or they used to get jumped bad you know. But they wouldn't say nothing, you know; they'd just take care of it on their own you know. . . . A lot of guys [in my Hoyo Maravilla clique], you know, they figured the older ones didn't hardly do anything, you know; they used to say so, you know. A lot of [older] guys wouldn't say nothing, you know what I mean, but you could look at the guys, you know, when you hang around with them you see all these stab wounds, and stuff.

If control is the expressed gang norm about fighting, how did this escalation of violence occur? Is it an erratic happenstance, depending on the personalities of boys at any given time? We asked, "How did you personally feel about fighting?" and found that only 20 percent expressed the gang norm and were "ready for a fight if necessary." Seventeen percent actively disliked fighting. A third, however, claimed that they enjoyed fighting. These are the boys in the thick of any gang fight, like this older Maravilla man who had youthful ambitions to become a boxer:

[How did you personally feel about fighting?] I loved it, loved it. I was one of the first ones in. I liked to throw blows. . . . [How important was the gang to you—very important, somewhat important, not important?] Somewhat important. [?] Well really, it was only when

they were going to fight, or, you know, like a hit-up or something,
you know, you're going to fight against another gang. They always
used to call me and all that, because I used to know how to punch. . . .
I put down my life for them for numerous of times, that's how I got
shot—five times—and knifed.

Some members recognized that fighting filled important psychological
needs, like this younger Maravilla woman: "At first I was afraid to fight
when I first joined the gang. But when I had a challenge and beat it, I was
overwhelmed. I never thought I could be that good in fighting. I felt I was
like—an overcomer, or something, for once." Sometimes the pressure
to fight came not only from the gang but from family members, as with
this older Maravilla woman:

> I used to fight a lot when I was young. Every afternoon I think I
> was the main event. Every afternoon. There was times when I was
> scared to fight, but I used to fight, because if I didn't fight and I didn't
> win my sister would beat the shit out of me when I got home, or my
> cousins they would hit me, you know. [They didn't like you to lose.]
> No, I couldn't lose. They didn't care how punched up I came home. I
> had to be a winner. That was the motto we had, you know, and if they
> beat you up you don't cry, you don't say nothing, you don't snivel.

There is no relationship between the number of deaths in a clique and
the number of members who really loved to fight. Apparently in a group
that expects to fight, the presence of more—or fewer—members who
personally enjoy fighting (as compared to the more reluctant warriors)
does not affect the outcome.

However, there is a gang value that may serve as a counternorm to the
norm of control. Cliques with a higher number of deaths were more likely
to have had more members who described themselves as *loco* or *muy
loco* (crazy) when they were in the gang.[10] *Locura* is the "craziness" or
wildness that is stereotypically associated with Chicano gangs and their
vatos locos (crazy guys). One of the older White Fence members defined
locura situationally, and solely in terms of aggressiveness in gang fights:

> I would consider muy loco two guys from my clique: Johnny and
> Bobo. We'd go out on a raid and these two guys would be jumping
> out of the cars before the cars were stopped and just whaling into

the group that's standing there. We always thought these guys were nuts. They had a competition thing—who was going to be first. But in any other situation these guys were very stable guys, very levelheaded.

Some of the most notable fighters become what gang members call "legends," like this legendary fighter from the first clique of White Fence: "Moto could stand against anybody. They still talk about him in the County Jail. They jumped him in the County Jail. He was the only one [from our neighborhood] in there. They jumped him and they couldn't down him. He was still standing when they backed off of him. They still talk about it."

In fact, most male members—and especially the younger ones—said that they were loco or muy loco. But locura meant different things for different members. The most common definition referred to generally unrestrained conduct. "I was muy loco. [?] I would take any kind of trouble. I was ready to fight; I was doing all the crazy things as much as I could." Another man answered, "*Muy loco*. [?] Because I used to get involved in all kinds of activities—getting drunk, getting loaded, going with broads, fighting—and you have to be *real* crazy to do something like that!" The definition applied to women as well as men, as this White Fence woman recalled: "I mean things didn't really matter. I mean nobody could explain anything. First we would just go and do it. We wouldn't even think, you know. We would just go and do it, just to do it, you know. And then we would go and get in trouble and we'd think about it later on. We're *pendejas* (stupid) for doing it, you know."

There was a notable increase: 81 percent of the men active in the 1970s described themselves in such terms, as compared with 65 percent of the men active in the 1950s. Women were at least as likely to define themselves as "loco" (80 percent), but not as muy loco.

But definitions tended to change over time. Older men tended to talk more about their locura as just going along with the guys: "I was just loco, I guess. [?] I used to do things the other [Hoyo Maravilla] guys would do, you know. I guess I wanted recognition, you know. Like the life-style, you know. Part of life in the barrio you know." And many of the older women reflected rather traditional values: "I was a little bit loca, but not real loca either. I wasn't real rowdy. I mean I respected my elders. If there was older people around I'd watch myself. I was taught respect."

By contrast, men who had been active in the 1970s were significantly more likely to emphasize violence in their self descriptions. Vigil (1988c) argues that the more extreme locos in a gang, often the more troubled youth, are the members who act as "instigators" of fights. Thus fights often started when boys got jumped by a rival gang and then called on their gang friends to retaliate. Such "instigators" were frowned upon, as this Maravilla man indicates, but clearly they had an effect.

> [OK, like you said you wouldn't be the kind to instigate or nothing like that?] I would never be an instigator, no. Hey if they jump me, you know, hey I just look at it, hey they're paying me back for the things I did to them, you know. I never reported it [to the gang]. I never was the snivelling type. A lot of guys say "Hey, homes, the vatos from over here jumped me," you know what I mean, "Let's go get them," you know, and I was never the type to say things like that, you know. I always took care of things on my own, you know what I mean? I figure I'm better off that way.

Instigators violated the gang norm of control, of "never starting fights but being willing to fight if necessary." Sometimes they were expelled from the gang: "This guy, he was a nut. He was always a troublemaker. He'd go out to other neighborhoods and start fights, and tell them he was from White Fence and then come back and tell us these guys were jumping on him. He was out there initiating the hassles. Always willing to start fights and stir the pot up. But we weren't tolerating any of his bullshit. So he got kicked out of the neighborhood." The value applied just as much to women's cliques, as a White Fence woman recalled:

> She used to start trouble and she couldn't back it up. I remember one time when we almost got our butts kicked. See when we were in Ramona [High School], we were like neutral. And she was going to Roosevelt [High School] and one time at lunchtime she went [to Ramona] and crossed out all the neighborhoods [graffitti] and she put "White Fence." And then she took off. And in the school there were only about six of us [from White Fence] and about a hundred other girls. And could you imagine when we went back to lunch? Everybody was thinking, "Ah, White Fence, they want to take over." And they were giving us all these dirty looks. . . . So she went

back to Roosevelt and she told the girls [from White Fence] what happened, so they said, "Hey we got to go back." . . . So after school, when we came out, . . . we heard somebody calling "Hey, homegirls!" and there were two carloads of girls—a truck and a station wagon. The teachers called the cops, and they told us to walk out, and so we walked out and they said, "Go to your friends, and get in the cars." . . . When we found out what happened we had a confrontation, and my sister and a couple of girls got her and beat her up.

In general the elevated level of violence over time had some relationship to each clique's sense that it must outdo its predecessor and also with some elements of the changing definitions of locura. Violence also puts the gang under considerable strain. This is a consequence of the "code of the barrio." In part, this translates into a norm that homeboys back one another up in all situations, especially fights. Thus Sweeney (1980) believes that this "code of the barrio" is one of the prime sources of lethal violence, especially in more recent times when guns replaced one-on-one fighting to establish a pecking order. Virtually all of these men acknowledged that they were "all for their barrio" when they were in the gang.

What happens when a boy *fails* to back up his homeboys? Slightly more than half of the men mentioned somebody who had been expelled from the clique, usually either because he ran from a fight or he was a police informer. The more violent cliques are no more likely to have expelled a member.

However, when we asked if the respondent knew of somebody who *should* have been kicked out, we found that the more violent cliques were significantly more likely to feel that an offender was improperly let off the hook.[11] (About a third of the men mentioned such cases.) A younger White Fence man remembered his resentment when asked if he knew anyone who deserved to get kicked out of the clique but was not: "Oh yeah. [Why weren't they kicked out?] He wasn't kicked out. I don't know. He left a homeboy hanging. The homeboy got cut. About seventy times. Almost died. [So you don't know why he wasn't kicked out?] Personally I don't understand it."

It is very difficult to expel a member while a gang is actively involved in fighting and being harassed by police, because an expulsion invariably involves a cleavage.

The guys that told him to get out were Bobo, Peter, and Alex and he said he would get out. They were all levelheaded dudes, and they weren't into accepting this bullshit that this guy had been doing. It's important who they were [i.e., that they were respected White Fence leaders]. But then he came back. And one of the guys went at him and he split. So it wasn't an easy thing. But the guys that were there at the time moved him out even though he didn't want to go out. [Did he live in the neighborhood?] Yeah he lived in the neighborhood. He was one of the originals. But he was still getting kicked out.

Even if the offense is serious, the offender has friends, and the gang must be in complete agreement about the expulsion or face a debilitating internal fight. In one case, it took several months of discussion before the gang expelled a member, and even then some of his friends stuck by him. A clique that is actively involved in fighting cannot afford this internal dissension. Members of the more violent cliques are all too aware that the fights may in fact demand their lives.

But the escalation in violence between 1950 and 1970 does not mean that there has been a continuous and inevitable rise in violence from clique to clique ever since the gang began. After a decade or more of escalation, gang killings in East Los Angeles dropped sharply in the 1980s (Baker, 1988). Why? Gang warfare is not the only problematic activity in a neighborhood. Drug use and marketing are important in many neighborhoods and affect the level of gang fighting. Older members argue that when heroin was introduced in the late 1940s gang warfare dipped sharply. Members of rival gangs crossed into each other's territories with impunity in search of heroin connections. Similarly, in the 1980s, neighborhood producers of PCP reputedly made efforts to curb gang activity in their own neighborhoods to ward off the attentions of police. The spread of heroin use has its own effect in reducing incentives for gang violence. However, some drugs, like PCP, cocaine, and crack, have psychopharmaceutical effects that enhance violence, and researchers have argued that most drug-related violence is centered on drug dealing that is not at all related to gangs (Goldstein et al., 1987).

Thus enhanced drug use and dealing in a neighborhood may have mixed effects on the overall level of violence. Our concern here is with its effects on intergang warfare. One older Maravilla man, for example, commented wryly that the gang's source of pride was no longer connected to fighting, but to drug use: "*La bandera* [the gang flag] is who can stay loaded longest now."

In addition, we cannot discount the effects of decades of efforts (both government-sponsored and grass roots) to curb gang warfare in these barrios. Gang programs began in the 1940s, shortly after the zoot-suit riots, and were an on-again-off again affair ever after. One of our Maravilla respondents had worked for a state-sponsored program designed to end violence by hiring gang members themselves as mediators (see Chapter Three). His response to a question about changes in the level of violence reflected both the enhanced drug marketing scene of the mid-1980s and his view of his own program:

> [Do you think the barrio is more or less violent now than when you were active?] Probably less violent. [And why do you say that?] A lot of them are into drugs you know. Drugs [i.e., heroin] cuts everybody, slows them down you know. The drug traffic is so high right now, you know, the guys they ain't got time for fighting, really, you know. All they have time for is "Hey man" you know, "Get high," you know what I mean. And then, you know, with all these gang projects, you know, a lot of guys, you know, are slacking off, man, trying to cut down, you know what I mean. [Less violent because there's gang workers working, right? That would help?] More community workers working with the gangs, you know, trying to cut down the violence, you know. I think it has been a big, a great success, you know, me personally. That's a personal opinion, though. . . . Once in a while you hear about [a killing], not too often any more. [OK, there's not too much gang banging[12] in the neighborhood now, right?] Nah, if anything happens it's over drugs, now, mostly.

Regrettably, the decline in lethal violence was rather short-lived, and once again, in the late 1980s and early 1990s, members of these gangs were killing one another. One rueful ex-member felt it was because the newest, youngest gang members just hadn't had direct experience with homeboys dying: They were willing to start the cycle all over again. Whether it was cyclical, related to drugs, or related to programs, violence seems to be endemic to these gangs.

Summary

This chapter raised questions about how the gangs as quasi-institutions might have changed with regard to socialization to deviance—especially to drug use, gender-role behavior, and violence. There are mixed answers. The data about joining the gang clearly indicates that the gangs of the 1970s were substantially more institutionalized than the gangs of the 1950s. Thus they probably exerted more influence over their members, irrespective of whatever else was happening in the community. And it is clear that drugs were used more, and more drugs were used in the 1970s than in the 1950s. The drug subculture of the gang was entrenched as never before. But it is not clear that gender relations were more exploitative in the 1970s than in the 1950s: In both epochs there was a strong double standard of behavior and considerable sexism. Finally, the cliques of the 1970s were active—and violent—during the peak of gang violence in East Los Angeles. There was substantial variation in levels of interclique violence, and much of this seemed to be related to gang-specific values. However, it should not be forgotten that intergang violence actually declined sharply among the cliques of the 1980s.

What does this mean for my initial questions? I took as an initial premise that the gang is the rowdiest of the adolescent cliques in the community, and that between the 1950 and the 1970s there had been a nationwide increase in "rowdiness" among all adolescent groups. The gangs of the 1970s were more institutionalized and more isolated from conventional influences than the gangs of the 1950s, and were clearly more deviant in drug use and in violence.

But the gang members were also tied socially to the conventional world. The conventional community exerts many kinds of controls over what it defines as deviant behavior. And that is the subject of Chapter 5.

chapter five

Gang Members and the World Around Them

That teenage gang members are linked to conventional barrio life is obvious. In fact, much of the members' time is spent with the family, at school, under the eyes of neighbors who are decidedly "square," and, sometimes, with conventional friends or dates. This linkage is usually overlooked in researchers' preoccupation with the life of the gang during the hours that it bands together. In Chapter Four I explored the influence of the gang; in this chapter I look at conventional agents of socialization.

We can understand only a little bit of this interaction from what the gang members have to say about their square contacts. Retrospective data like this may reflect romanticism about the old days, ruefulness at missed opportunities to reintegrate with the conventional world, or self-righteousness at having "gotten out in time." But what evidence we have indicates that the cliques of the 1950s were more closely integrated with the conventional barrio structures and norms. The cliques of the 1970s appear more remote, and faced more disapproval and more efforts at control.

Did Neighbors Oppose the Gang?

We start with how these respondents recalled neighbors' reactions to the gang. Earlier we discussed the predecessors of the gangs themselves. Those barrio youth groups appear to have been accepted by the conventional families in the neighborhood—especially those associated with the Purissima church in White Fence. When we put all of the members of the four earlier cliques together, though, we include some cliques that were heavily involved with drugs and fighting. They had clearly moved beyond the limits of community acceptance as neighborhood youth groups. They were gangs, and were defined as such in the neighborhood. This affected our earlier cliques.

But the gang norm continued to insist that, since the gang was "all for the neighborhood," the neighborhood must be "all for the gang," or at the worst, neutral. Thus 61 percent of the men from the earlier cliques felt that the neighbors were neutral toward them, and 26 percent felt that they were favorable while only 13 percent felt that they were negative. Girls were under fewer illusions about their own status. Only 39 percent of the older women felt that neighbors were neutral, 22 percent felt that they were positive, and 39 percent felt that they were negative. One older White Fence man expressed his view of the neighbors: "We were accepted for the simple reason we took care of the people in the neighborhood—older people, friends. They used to look up to us.

For one man from a more recent clique in El Hoyo Maravilla, the value of integration into the neighborhood persisted, and may well have been supported by experiences with a few particular families:

Like they would help us out, talk to us. We would help them. That was a long time ago, but you know now it's different. [You said you would also help them, right?] Yeah. [Help them, like the older people?] Like kids, like if you see one running around the streets, you get him and take him home, help the ladies with their packages to the house, cut their lawns, carry the trash out. That was when we were growing up.

But a quarter of the younger men were more likely to acknowledge that neighbors were hostile to their clique. Even though a majority continued to feel that neighbors were either neutral or favorably inclined, an increased proportion in both neighborhoods recognized sharp conflicts:

[Neighbors?] Ah man, they couldn't stand you. [Negative, positive?] Negative. [Could you give me an example?] Oh, "You're a cholo, you're a chump; you're no good for nothing," you know what I mean. [They didn't want you around?] Right. "Troublemaker," they label you, you know what I mean; bad influence person. [They called you names, like cholos, right?] Yeah, they'd call us punks, and stuff, you know what I mean. We just let it go, you know what I mean. We'd tell them, "Ah, shove it in your ear," you know what I mean. We'd cuss them out.

Younger women concurred: "Oh those in the neighborhood that didn't have no family [in the gang], they were very negative. [?] Name-calling, like 'You girls are up to no good. You're going to end up tramps.' My neighbors would all say if you're from a gang right away you're symbolized as no good. Right away you're bad. And that wasn't true." And with the large Monstros/Monstras clique of White Fence (active in the 1970s and 1980s) a few members made no pretense at neighborhood altruism: they were quite aware that they intimidated neighbors, like this Monstra: "[The neighbors] didn't bother us. They didn't get in the way, and like they would see us walking by they would stay in the yard."

Did Parents Oppose the Gang?

When we asked about how their parents reacted to their membership in the gang, a similar pattern of generational difference emerges. In the earlier cliques only about a third of men and women reported that their parents were upset at their joining a gang, and an additional quarter of the men reported their parents just didn't say anything. In some cases there were special circumstances, as with this older Maravilla man:

They didn't approve, really, but they never said too much about it. [?] A lot of them were too old. They were getting too old in their life, so they were losing their strength. They couldn't deal with us. Plus they had the problems of having to feed us, clothe us, and keeping a roof over our heads because of the times, the hard times that were there at the time. So hey, they—I know they didn't approve of us belonging to a gang, but like I say, they were getting weak and old so they accepted some of it, you know.

And a woman from one of the earlier White Fence cliques, whose parents neglected her and who had been an incest victim, commented: "My mother didn't even know that I was in. [?] My father even less. He didn't know either. They didn't care where I used to go." Most of these parents, however, were Mexican-born and were less inclined to define their children's activities in terms of dangerous gangs. There was an exception to this—the girls who dressed like *pachucas,* with exaggerated pompadour hairstyles and short skirts. One of the older White Fence women remembered: "My mother used to feel embarrassed with me when I used to go out on the street with her—especially downtown—because, you know, white people would look at the way I was dressed and my mother thought I was a punk."

By contrast with this relative indifference in the older generation, most of the parents of recent clique members were born in the United States, and very aware of what was going on, and particularly of the well-established patterns of drug abuse. By contrast, in the recent cliques almost two-thirds of the men and women (double the proportion in earlier cliques) reported their parents were upset. The gang reputation for violence and "trouble" seems to have been paramount in parents' reactions. Here are two younger men:

> My folks didn't like it. They didn't like the idea of gangs. [?] Well, she didn't like it because she didn't want me to get hurt.

> They didn't like it, you know. They didn't like any of the guys. They didn't want us to get in trouble; they wanted us to stay out of it. They didn't want us to go to jail or anything like that. [That would be more if something had happened?] Yeah, something would happen, and they would yell at us, you know, not to be in a gang, *verdad?* They didn't want us to be out in the streets. They didn't want us to be fighting.

Some younger respondents also recall their parents' helplessness. This younger White Fence man, born in Mexico, reported his widowed mother's impotence:

> By the time I was already in, I was already into gang banging, she was usually already at work, so she was always at work, so she couldn't really. . . . By the time I was into gang banging and was a gang member, it was already too late. Well, I wouldn't bring them home, you know—I would just, you know— [She knew?] Yeah, from the neighbors. They would always see me with the guys. But there was really nothing she could do, really nothing she could do. I was already in the neighborhood, in the gang.

A surprisingly large proportion, especially of members active in the 1950s, were able to conceal their membership from their parents—17 percent of the older men, compared with 9 percent of younger men, and 33 percent of older women, compared with 22 percent of younger women. Membership in a notorious local gang can be concealed because parents are working, are preoccupied with a large family, and often just believe that their child is out playing with one of the numerous other adolescent groups in the neighborhood. As one older man said, simply, "My folks were unaware. I wouldn't never bring anyone to the house but one person."

While very few respondents said that their parents approved of the gang, a significant fraction—especially in the earlier cliques—said that their parents liked and approved of the *kids* that were in the gang. Many parents made judgments only about the kids that they met. One older man said, "My folks were—they reacted OK. I mean, like I said, most of the guys were nice guys. They would come over the house; my mother would talk to them and everything, so she knew all of them, so, she never—she didn't really react bad to the guys." And another said, "She liked my friends. Some of them. [But the ones she knew, she approved?] Oh yeah. [?] Because they were very respectful to her." Ironically, some respondents recognized that their parents' apparent approval was a not-very-well-concealed effort to retain control over the kids, like this man from one of the recent cliques. His mother had grown up with a brother in the White Fence gang, and she felt that if she could keep her eye on the boys, she had a chance of controlling them: "[My mother was] positive, I guess. [?] Because everybody used to hang around at my house, in the back yard, and my mother, she used to feed everybody, you know. [?] Mother knew them all; she used to feed them all. She made sure we stood in the yard." Another woman from a recent White Fence clique reported that her grandmother made a similar effort: "My grandmother she used to tell me, 'You want to be doing that stuff, you do it in your room. You want to be out there late at night—just till a certain time. Don't come home too late. And don't you be doing bad things.' Things that I was doing she didn't know. But she used to let me bring my girlfriends in the house and play records."

The emphasis on "respect" in these quotations is characteristic of the demands made on young people for behavior toward their elders.

Older gang members recall that not only would they demand that their gang friends act respectfully when they were visiting, but they would also censure a fellow gang member if he was disrespectful to an older relative on the streets. Thus the gang's reputation and self-image for acceptable behavior was maintained by the fact that traditional standards of behavior established in the family were often extended to most of the neighborhood.

Did Nongang Age-Mates Oppose the Gang?

Next to neighbors and family come age-mates. Overwhelmingly, these men and women hung out more with gang than with nongang friends, in both older and younger cliques. However, about half of these gang members also had close friends who were not in the gang. It bears reiterating that gang members are not isolated from other adolescents in their communities. Significantly more of the men in earlier cliques had such friends—65 percent, compared with 34 percent of men in more recent cliques, indicating that the male gang members, at least, became more socially isolated in recent years. There were no such "generational" differences among women.

And, given the focus on the gang, it is not surprising that 75 percent of the women—and especially the younger women—had boyfriends who were in the gang, and only 43 percent dated boys that were square. However, it was different for boys: It *is* surprising that only a minority of either the older or the younger men—40 percent—took their girlfriends from the gang and 65 percent of the men dated square girlfriends.

What was the reaction to square dates? How were they different from dates with gang boys or girls? While more than a quarter of the girls who dated square boys said they were "nicer," and another quarter said they were more "respectful," many girls—almost a quarter— that dated square boys recall being bored. An older White Fence woman reminisced: "I had a boyfriend that was square once. [?] He was very polite. He would open the door when I would go in, and he would call me yes ma'am and no ma'am. And I couldn't stand it! I was used to the homeboys, you know." Square boyfriends also tried to control the girls' behavior—and especially the stigmatizing *chola* makeup: "My boyfriend didn't like [my being in White Fence]. He said, 'If you ever shave your eyebrows off and wear eyelashes I'll divorce you. I'll leave you.'"

By contrast, many of the boys, reflecting the traditionalism that underlay their sexist attitudes toward girls in gangs, enjoyed the experience of dating conventional girls. They were "nicer," "less streetwise," less likely to drink or use drugs. Square girls were their future, they hoped. They dressed differently from gang girls—and the chola style of dress and makeup was very stigmatizing. Even a well-behaved chola simply could not be introduced to respectable people. Three younger Maravilla men explicitly contrasted square dates with homegirls from the gangs:

> [What was different about going out with squares?] They knew how to act. [In what way?] Present themselves. I wouldn't take a homegirl to the house. I would take a square one to my house and introduce her to my grandmother. They dressed different; they looked different.

> In the beginning I just wanted to get into their pants, but as time went on I wanted to be with one of them because I figured out that if I was with a homegirl she would take drugs and drink and then I would do the same thing, and it wouldn't help me. But if I was with a square girl she would help me because she wouldn't drink, smoke, or do any of that stuff. So that's why in the end I went for them.

> Well, my girlfriends, my *rucas*—I never really cared for cholas, you know what I mean—they didn't like me to be in gangs either. I only went with one chola in my life, because I didn't really like them. They're—they're a piece [of ass]. [?] Because you know you had a good woman, you know what I mean. . . . The cholas man, hey, all they knew was shit, what was doing around, and you didn't want them to know that. [What was different about going out with squares?] OK, you know they were going to be good. You know they going to take care of business and in the house, be a good housewife, you know what I mean.

Many square girlfriends tried to influence these gang members, often trying to get them to leave the gang. Men from recent cliques were distinctly more likely to report that their girlfriends disapproved of the gang—half, as compared with only 17 percent of the men active in earlier cliques. Again, it was different for girls: only 16 percent of the women (older and younger) reported that their boyfriends disapproved of their being in a gang. Their boyfriends, of course, were predominantly gang boys. Thus conventional dating partners influenced the men, and in particular the younger men, more than they influenced the women. Men in general were more likely to date outside the gang, and younger men were more likely to have girlfriends that actively discouraged their gang activities.

In sum, neighbors, family, and—for the men—girlfriends all tended to have been more actively opposed to gang membership in recent cliques as compared with older cliques. The gangs of the 1970s, then, were operating both with less involvement with square friends and in a climate of disapproval: They were defined as deviant groups, and conventional neighbors, parents, and girl/boyfriends tried to discourage membership. It is clear that boys, at least, were still in touch with the "square" world and still responsive to it. Girls may have been in a more problematic situation, more fully absorbed by their membership in an increasingly deviant group, and not even aware how deviant they were even in the eyes of their fellow—male—gang members.

Salience of the Gang

Efforts at exerting control over deviance, however, must be placed in the context of how salient the gang was to the boys and girls. For most, the gang was "very important." As Vigil comments, for some gang members "egos become submerged in the barrio [gang] and its activities" (Vigil, 1988b:429). This was especially true for boys, even though men from more recent cliques were even more likely to see the gang as "very important" than were older men. Overall more than three-quarters put the gang in this category. For a few, this meant comparatively mild peer-group attachment, like this older Maravilla man: "It was very important. [?] Because I had good friends. [Very important because you had good friends and—] We had a good time. Went to a lot of parties together. Had good times at parties." But many men expressed total dedication to the gang, which was often even more important than family.

> To me it was my life, my one and only way. [What do you mean, "your life"?] My only mission . . . [You were all for your barrio? Could you please tell me how you felt?] Well, I felt that was the only thing going for me. It was my neighborhood. They were like my brothers and

sisters. I mean, at that time, that's the only thing I had. It was them and my grandparents.

It was the most important thing in my life at that time. There was nothing that came even close to it except maybe my own personal family. But even then at the time there was no problems at the home, so my gang life was my one love.

All my life. Very important. [?] Because it meant my life. I was a dedicated member. Very, very important. [?] I lived there, and it was—I'd say I lived there, I'll tell you. [?] All day and all night.

This sense of total dedication was also significantly and substantially greater among the women from recent cliques than among the women active in the 1950s. Among the women from earlier cliques, only half felt that the gang was "very important," but a full 79 percent of the younger women expressed this kind of dedication. The contrast is illustrated by the different responses of one older and three younger White Fence women:

[How important was the gang?] Not very important. Like I saw it it was just a bunch of good friends getting together and for some reason or another—well, I mean, you know, the guys used to see us coming and they started calling us "Honeys," you know, and then they just gave us that name. That's when it all started.

At that time I didn't have nobody or anything. I was always at my neighborhood, always with the girls and try to make myself look bad and stuff, you know, yelling it out and stuff.

The year that I was there it was like, umm, they were like family, because we would all take care of each other. . . . I think they were like my own family. I think I was more with them than my own family, because I left them for a while.

It was very important. Because that's all I had to look forward to, was my neighborhood, you know. That's all. It was my people—my neighborhood, my homies, my homeboys, my homegirls—that was everything to me. That was everything, you know. It wasn't all about my *familia;* it was all about my homeboys and homegirls.

The fact that the gang was psychologically more significant to more of the younger people than to older—especially women—gives special poignancy to the fact that neighbors, family, and girlfriends were more likely to be exerting stronger efforts at social control. Ironically, their efforts were less likely to succeed for the younger people.

Summary: The Meaning of Change

It is plain that the gangs show signs of evolution as deviant groups. In their earliest cliques, these two barrio groups worked out what Fine (1987) calls "normal adolescent deviance" within the context of traditional expectations for neighborhood male groups. They were apparently accepted as such within their communities. But even in the early days, following World War II (especially as far as female gang membership was concerned), these "rowdy" community groups were showing somewhat more deviance.

By the 1970s, the gangs had shifted further in the direction of deviance. Even though gang membership was not passed on from father to son in the media-stereotyped sense, gang membership became more of a family matter in the 1970s than in the 1950s. Older boys and girls were coming in, and some of the cliques were lasting longer. There was more drug use during party sociability, and among the boys, more exaggerated acting out of masculine roles than in the earlier groups. There was more lethal violence, and there were more members who adopted a violence-oriented version of the gang norm of wildness, or locura. More of the younger men and women felt that neighbors and parents opposed their membership, and more of the younger men felt that their girlfriends were opposed. Fewer members in recent cliques had friends outside of the gang. The gang was operating more in a climate of disapproval, and, perhaps not surprisingly, the gang appears to have been psychologically salient to more of the members active in the 1970s than to the men and women of the earlier period. Despite a climate of increased liberality toward women, there are no indications that women who joined the gangs in the 1970s were any more accepted as peers than were women who joined in the 1950s.

What portion of this increased deviance is a matter of a general cultural shift toward greater "normal deviance"? We have no way of saying, of course. Clearly, though, a good deal of this increase has to do with the nature of the gang as a quasi-institution, with the nature of inter-clique aspirations, with the nature of local myths and legends, and with the nature of gang values and norms as they have developed over time. These are not irreversible, though, as the reduction in gang violence during the 1980s clearly demonstrates. The gangs are not isolated from all conventional influence even as quasi-institutions, any more than any individual member is isolated from conventional influence.

While these gangs have been quasi-institutionalized for decades, they have not, by any means, taken over their barrios and intimidated the conventional residents. This directly refutes the media portrait of gang neighborhoods. Nor are these communities the disorganized and demoralized underclass deserts that some researchers find in certain Puerto Rican neighborhoods in New York.

One final note. At the outset of my discussion of control, at the end of Chapter Three, I mentioned the view of some researchers that gangs are oppositional, if not potentially revolutionary, and in any event somehow articulated with class. Youth groups like the gangs that are at the rowdy end of the continuum of normal adolescent deviance are involved with what one English researcher calls a "guerrilla warfare" against the alien bourgeois culture of the schools, a resistance movement, in effect (Corrigan, 1979).

This view differs from the kind of normal deviance that Fine talks about. Gangs openly defy the norms. This is not the covert and secretive deviance of the "respectable" Little Leaguers. This culture encourages its members to openly subvert and defy the norms and ideals of the schools, even though in the earlier days the Chicano gangs accepted and did *not* harass the scholarly bookworms among their peers. But, as Willis (1981) points out, this very culture of defiance in effect dooms the boys at best to jobs just like those their fathers hold, and transfers the defiant and subversive attitude from school to workplace. The gang becomes good socialization for lower-level working jobs. At worst it becomes effective socialization for prison and the prison aftermath of labor-market marginality.

The thing that has changed now, however, is that many of those lower-level jobs that young gang members used to obtain in the 1950s are gone. The men have different careers, as we shall see in a later chapter. But first we will look at the gang members' families of origin.

▲▼ chapter six ▲▼▲▼▲▼▲▼▲▼▲

Gang Members' Families

Most boys and girls in East Los Angeles never became involved
with gangs. Because the community has so many problems, over the
years researchers have been tempted to search for the roots of gang
involvement in some special characteristics of the members' families.
After all, *something* must make these particular young people susceptible
to the attractions of this most rowdy of youth groups. Where better to
search than in the family?

This search has taken three major approaches. The oldest emphasized some structural feature: thus it is said that immigration and poverty
cause family stress, and family stress weakens controls. Thrasher noted
the general fragility of social controls in immigrant neighborhoods of
1920s Chicago, and the particular "failure of the immigrant [family] to
control [its] children" (1927:489). This concern with immigrant family
problems was regularly applied to Chicano gangs (see Griffith, 1948).
Most recently Vigil (1988a), in his concept of "multiple marginality,"
broadened it. He maintained that large segments of the Mexican-origin
population suffered from economic and ecological marginality and from
culture conflict, as well. Under these circumstances, family controls
often lost out to street socialization. People who could not adapt began
to generate a marginalized cholo subculture. Gangs express the essence
of this cholo subculture, and youngsters from troubled families are particularly likely to join them. A similar general approach is taken by researchers who argue that stresses suffered by poverty-stricken parents
combine with the constraints imposed by limited resources to create
"maladaptive parenting" (Garbarino, Schellenbach, and Sebes, 1986).

A second approach searches for a subcultural foundation for gang involvement. One of the early contentions was that family socialization to a special working-class subculture generates and sustains male gang activity (Miller, 1958). And more recently Moore and Vigil (1987) suggest that once cholos marry and have children of their own, whole families are embedded in the cholo subculture.

A third approach emphasizes psychological problems stemming from the family. A Freudian stance pervaded much of the early literature on juvenile delinquency (see Aichhorn, 1935), and when it was applied to gangs, broken homes began to receive considerable attention (Shaw and McKay, 1931; Slawson, 1926; Glueck and Glueck, 1934).[1] This psychological tradition has consistently asserted that delinquency is largely a reaction to frustrating and emotionally disturbing conditions at home (Healy and Bronner, 1936; Reckless, Dinitz, and Kay, 1957). In fact, one leading scholar contended that a poor self-concept, generated in the family, creates the critical psychological vulnerability to delinquent solutions (Dinitz, Scarpitti, and Reckless, 1962). Vigil (1988a) echoes much the same argument with specific reference to Chicano gangs. Gang membership in adolescence reinforces delinquent tendencies that have their roots in family stress during childhood.[2] Several researchers have explored factors in the family that insulate poverty-stricken youngsters from delinquency, and they repeatedly note the importance of the quality of family relationships—the emotional climate (see Werner, 1983).

In short, a concern with gang members' families has a long history. There is no question that most recent theorizing about juvenile delinquency—and gangs—has tended to emphasize the influence of larger systems, and thus to de-emphasize the intimate interactions within face-to-face groups. But families play a role in these broader approaches as well. Hagedorn (1988) claims that the recent appearance of gangs in a midwestern minority community is largely the result of economic changes that deprived minority workers of decent jobs and their communities of viable institutions. In particular, he notes that gang members' parents generally held decent jobs of the kind that the members themselves cannot obtain. This view contrasts sharply with the traditional view that gangs come from perennially poverty-stricken or marginalized families. Instead, Hagedorn posits a pattern of communitywide downward mobility—with all its attendant family stresses—in neighborhoods that are already hard-pressed.

In this chapter I deal with each of the major themes relating to the family—questions relating to immigration and ethnicity and to parental economic status, and questions about the emotional climate in the household during respondents' childhoods. The approach is descriptive, and our major interest is in the extent to which families of the earlier clique members reflect more—or fewer—features that have been defined as problems than families of more recent cliques. If one follows Thrasher's reasoning, one might expect that older—largely immigrant—families would have more problems. But if one follows Vigil's reasoning, one might expect that more recent families, increasingly "choloized," would have more problems.

Ethnicity and Poverty in the Families

Mexicanness

Whether "Mexicanness" can be seen as a problem depends on whether one expects strains to be associated with immigrant status and acculturation. We expected the families of members of earlier cliques to be far more "Mexican" than those of the recent ones, and they were, on all measures.

The first aspect was nativity. More than two-thirds of the parents of male members of earlier cliques were born in Mexico, compared with only a third or fewer of the parents of members of more recent cliques. Interestingly, the women gang members—even the ones from earlier cliques—were notably less likely to have Mexican-born parents. The women in more recent cliques were even less Mexican, with a minuscule 9 percent of parents born in Mexico.[3] About a third of the parents of more recent clique members—both men and women—were born in Los Angeles itself.

The second aspect was cultural. Of course, Spanish was the habitual language in many of the homes. In about 60 percent of the boys' families and 44 percent of the girls' families it was the language spoken every day, by both parents and children. (Households in the earlier cliques were no more or less likely than those in recent cliques to rely on Spanish, oddly enough.) In many of the homes, parents spoke in Spanish and children answered in English. English was the everyday language in only a small fraction of the households of earlier clique members, but in the more recent cliques, it was the normal language in 42 percent of the boys' homes and 61 percent of the girls' homes. Many of the parents, particularly of recent clique members, actively encouraged the use of Spanish.

We also asked a series of questions designed to give some indication about traditionalism in the family. Did the father set himself up as the head of the household, with no questions asked, in the traditional Mexican pattern? Did he let his wife drive the family car? Did he restrict his wife's visitors? Did he let his wife handle the money?

Generally speaking, households in the earlier cliques were more patriarchal and, generally speaking (not surprisingly, given the nativity patterns) boys' households were more patriarchal than girls'. The majority of boys' fathers in the earlier cliques made claims to patriarchal control and to exclusive use of the family car (if there was one), and a small minority (20 percent) attempted to control their wives' visitors. Ironically, more fathers in the earlier cliques ceded control over money matters to their wives.

The pattern was not quite so patriarchal in the women gang members' households. Only about half of the women's fathers tried to establish themselves as unequivocal heads of the household, and none tried to restrict their wives' visitors. They were also more likely to let their wives drive the family car. Many of the differences in perceived patriarchy between men's fathers in earlier and more recent cliques can be explained by nativity: Mexican-born fathers, both earlier and more recent, acted more like patriarchs.

These differences between girls' and boys' household traditionalism and Mexicanness are somewhat surprising.[4] It may simply be that the more culturally Mexican girls simply didn't join the gangs. Traditional Mexican families are intensely opposed to any kind of street involvement for girls. Many of the girls who joined the earlier cliques came from traditional Mexican households, but they tended to be sisters of the boys who were centrally involved, and we have discussed earlier the ways in which such girls were controlled by their families even if they were members of a gang.

Despite the fact that virtually all of these boys and girls were born in the United States, the family and community combined to make most of them feel Mexican when they were growing up. Not Mexican American, but Mexican. A woman from a recent clique traced the feelings to her family: "Mexican, I felt Mexican. Because both of my parents spoke in Spanish and I had an older sister that wasn't born from here. She was born in Mexico. I grew up knowing English but my mom and dad did speak Spanish in the household and she did tell us what our race was as we were growing up." A woman from one of the earlier cliques explained that her feelings about ethnicity had deeper roots in discrimination than in family processes: "I felt Mexican because [laugh] at a very tender age the white people let me know that my skin color was brown. Which was in Texas and they discriminated against me. And I knew I was Mexican, and after that I was very proud about it. That's why I had so many fights with the white people in San Fernando High and in junior high school because I refused to be put down because I was brown."

Ethnic identity confusion has been identified as a problem for Chicanos in all kinds of communities, and it is by no means confined to youngsters who join gangs or have other kinds of problems. A small minority—about 11 percent of the gang members from earlier cliques and 5 percent of those from recent cliques—admitted to feeling "confused" about their ethnic identity when they were growing up. It is more than likely that most people who said they felt Mexican actually experienced many of the feelings that were articulated well by one man from an earlier clique who acknowledged his ethnic identity confusion: "I was confused when I was growing up. [?] Well, because I couldn't speak English properly, the way I thought I should, the way they tried to teach me at school. I couldn't pick it up. And I was eating different food. I was taking tacos and everybody had sandwiches. And at that time in Marianna [school] they used to prohibit you from speaking Spanish. And that was my language." However, it is easy to make too much of such identity confusion. It was undoubtedly shared by other youngsters in the barrios: these gang members were by no means unusually Mexican for their times. In fact, given recent increases in immigration to East Los Angeles, the recent cliques of the gangs may actually be *less* Mexican than the general run of adolescents in these communities. Certainly, there is no indication in these data that Mexicanness or identity confusion led these youngsters into the gang.

Poverty: Household Composition and Mobility during Childhood

We developed several indicators of poverty in the household. Our respondents listed all household members and their jobs, and gave us other information about the household, in five-year intervals for their entire lifetimes. During their childhood, households in this sample were quite large, averaging 6 or 7 people (Table 6-1). Usually this meant that there were several brothers or sisters, but occasionally a grandparent or—rarely—a cousin or other relative was present. There was substantial variation in household size. Nine percent had only 3 people, including the respondent, while in 17 percent there were 10 or more people. Very few of the respondents (15 percent) could have a bedroom all to themselves: Most shared with same-sex siblings.

Most of the boys and girls in the earlier cliques grew up with both parents in the household, although fathers tended to disappear as the young people entered adolescence (Table 6-1). In the recent cliques, it was far more common for these homes to be hit by divorce or desertion when the respondents were quite young. This was particularly the case for the women's families. By their mid-teens, a sizable number—more than a third—of gang boys and girls were living in homes headed by their mothers. However, the majority had both parents, and, if we take seriously the data on patriarchy just presented, the households were not dominated by mothers, either.

There were not very many three-generation households. Occasionally a grandparent lived with the family, and very occasionally grandparents (or some other family member) took charge of the respondent, replacing absent or abusive parents. In sum, these households have more of the characteristics associated with poverty than with the traditional Mexican extended family.

Poverty: The Household Economy during Childhood

The parents of these gang members were generally poorly educated. Only about half of the respondents knew their parents' educational level, but in the earlier cliques, only about 10 percent of the fathers had completed high school, and in the more recent cliques the proportion was still lower than one-third. Fathers and mothers who were born in Mexico tended to be particularly poorly educated—especially in the earlier cliques, where more than half of the Mexican-born parents were functionally illiterate (with less than four years of school). Even in the more recent cliques, Mexican-born parents had little schooling. Twenty percent of the fathers and 14 percent of the mothers had no school at all. On the other end, 19 percent of the fathers and 22 percent of the mothers had completed high school.

And, generally, although fathers did not hold very good jobs, the jobs

Table 6-1. Household Composition during Childhood,
Earlier Cliques Compared with Recent Cliques

	When respondent was aged:		
	0–5	6–10	11–15
Male	a. Median household size		
Earlier Cliques	6.0	7.5[a]	7.0
Recent Cliques	5.0	6.0[a]	7.0
Female			
Earlier Cliques	6.0	7.0	7.0
Recent Cliques	6.0	7.0	7.0
Male	b. Father was present		
Earlier Cliques	82.6%	82.6%	71.7%
Recent Cliques	73.3	76.7	63.3
Female			
Earlier Cliques	77.8	83.3	61.1
Recent Cliques	57.6	69.7	63.6
Male	c. Mother was present		
Earlier Cliques	93.5%	91.3%	87.0%
Recent Cliques	95.0	95.0	88.3
Female			
Earlier Cliques	94.4	94.4	94.4
Recent Cliques	97.0	87.9	87.9
Male	d. Grandfather was present		
Earlier Cliques	6.5%	8.7%	6.5%
Recent Cliques	8.3	8.3	8.3
Female			
Earlier Cliques	5.6	5.6	5.6
Recent Cliques	9.1	6.1	9.1
Male	e. Grandmother was present		
Earlier Cliques	6.5%	13.0%	8.7%
Recent Cliques	18.3	15.0	13.3
Female			
Earlier Cliques	22.2	22.2	22.2
Recent Cliques	9.1	9.1	9.1

[a] Kendall's tau significant > .05

were better for fathers of the more recent clique members than of the earlier ones. More fathers of earlier clique members were unskilled (33 percent compared with 9 percent in recent cliques), reflecting the higher proportion of Mexican-born workers. In the recent cliques there were more semiskilled factory workers (53 percent compared with 36 percent in the earlier cliques) or skilled workers (35 percent compared with 29 percent in the earlier cliques). There were few differences between boys' fathers and girls' fathers.

There were, however, interesting gender differences in whether the mothers stayed at home, following traditional role prescriptions, or whether they worked. For both boys and girls, mothers in the earlier cliques were distinctly more likely to be housewives. But in both earlier and more recent cliques, the boys' mothers were much more likely to be at home and the girls' mothers to be working as a matter of course. Specifically, in the earlier cliques 19 percent of the boys' mothers and 44 percent of the girls' mothers were working, and in the recent cliques 37 percent of the boys' mothers and 56 percent of the girls' mothers were working. Mothers' jobs were strictly for cash—and largely factory work.

Were these gang members from desperately poor families? Probably so, by middle-class standards. However, subjectively, most respondents (61 percent) felt they were no poorer than most other people in the barrio, while 15 percent felt that their families were "better off," and only 24 percent felt that they were poorer than most people. Though these were generally poor barrios, most of the gang members did not feel that they were among the poorest of the poor. Slightly more than a third (37 percent) owned their own homes. A quarter lived in very small homes, with four rooms or less, but 10 percent grew up in homes with eight or more rooms, even though (judging by local housing characteristics) the rooms probably were very small.

Perhaps even more important than poverty per se, it is important to realize that gang members—especially in the earlier cliques—grew up in households in which at least one and often more than one person worked. In only a handful of male members' households was nobody working. When fathers were present, it was fathers who worked. In more recent cliques, mothers entered the work force in significant numbers as the respondents grew older even when fathers were present. Brothers and sisters contributed to the family income in a quarter of the homes, and in about 8 percent grandparents also worked. Girls' homes were more frequently broken than boys'. There were higher proportions of girls' homes with no workers (up to 24 percent in the more recent cliques) and fewer fathers and more mothers worked.

Even though wages were the principal source of income in most of these households, respondents noted additional sources, as well. Nine percent of the men and 20 percent of the women recalled some other sources of income coming into the family when they were between the ages of 6 and 10. These include welfare, odd jobs, pensions and—rarely mentioned—illicit income (in 3 percent of the households). In their early teens, 30 percent of the men and 23 percent of the women listed other sources of income. Importantly, only 9 percent of the men and 6 percent of the women listed welfare. Increased proportions recorded their own income from illegal activities (9 percent of the boys in their early teens, rising to 27 percent in the later teens).

In most of these respects, these families probably differed very little from their neighbors. They were Mexican, they were large, they were working, they were poor. Occasionally the fathers departed, but the overall profile is not desperately poor, and there is a lot of variation. There is really very little support in these data for the notion that gang membership is generated by the strains of poverty and immigrant life. It is when we turn to the emotional climate of the family during childhood that problems begin to be evident.

Emotional Climate in the Family

Many of these families were not particularly happy, and in some cases they were acutely unhappy—at least in the reminiscences of these former gang members. Retrospective data about family relationships are tricky at best, and here we are dealing with men and women who may have been the family's "bad" boy or girl. Many still harbor unresolved feelings of bitterness toward their parents. However, whether the data we report here reflect the reality of family life or just the projections of unhappy men and women, these perceptions had an effect.

Relations between Parents

Our first set of questions asked about whether the parents were generally cheerful—or grouchy—and about how well the parents got along with each other. Slightly less than half of the men, but two-thirds of the

women, said that their fathers were reasonably happy. (Ten percent said
that they didn't know their fathers well enough to say.) Respondents
from earlier and more recent cliques saw their fathers pretty much the
same way.

"Happy" fathers were not much discussed. Most of the descriptions
of "grouchy" fathers (and even some of the "happy" ones) reflect both
the pressures and insecurities of hard manual labor and also the Mexican
masculine value of emotional reserve. Here are some of the men from
earlier cliques talking about their parents:

> My father was worn down and grouchy. [How about your mother?]
> Just worn down.

> My father was more or less grouchy; that would fit him. My dad
> wouldn't say too much, especially when he was sober. He was one of
> those persons that wouldn't say nothing. He'd say it all when he was
> drunk. . . . [How did your parents get along?] Well it all depended
> how things were going. If things were going all right, they'd get along
> good. If things were bad financially, there was problems.

> My father was grouchy. [Why was that?] Ignorance [laugh]. Because
> you know at that time men were ignorant. They never played with
> us or they never took us out or they never sat down and talked to
> us. . . . You know that—the father is always working. He comes
> home tired and he has no time for the kids. [I know, just work and
> come home; just provide. Try and provide and that's it, right?] That's
> it, just provide.

And some from recent cliques echo the same themes: One member said,
"My father was pretty much for working and quiet. He wasn't—[You
don't think he was grouchy? Or was he happy?] I'd say my dad was
pretty much happy. He was—you know, he'd let my mother take care of
the household." Another said, "My father was serious. He hardly ever
showed any kind of emotion." A woman from a recent clique recalled
her father with undisguised bitterness: "He was mean, selfish, tight. He
didn't know anything about understanding the way he had us living. . . .
When I was just 11, he used to come home and hit us when he would
come home drunk. We were always afraid. [Did he ever beat up on your

mother?] Yeah. I would say about four, five times a month. We would cry or try to defend her, fight back with my father."

A higher proportion of the respondents said that their mothers were happy—two-thirds of the men and 60 percent of the women, with no differences between respondents from earlier and more recent cliques. Again, the descriptions conform to traditional Mexican family role expectations, emphasizing the joys of motherhood and family security. An older man responded, "Oh, my mother was always happy. [Why was that?] Well, bringing us up, the family." A younger man commented, "My mother was happy. [Why was that?] Well my dad provided for her, you know. That was their main concern, you know." Another young man's response was "She was always happy. She was content to stay at home and look after our needs. For everything that we wanted she was always there."

Only about half of these men and women said that their parents got along well together. A fairly high proportion—especially in the recent cliques—saw their fathers beat their mothers occasionally. (Twenty percent of the men and women in the earlier cliques witnessed such battery, as did a third of the men and 40 percent of the women from recent cliques.) Only a small minority experienced this as a routine feature of their home life. This older man's story is fairly typical:

> Yeah, that happened—ah, once in a while. Sometimes when things were not going right for him, you know. It didn't happen every week, but it happened at least once a month. Like I say, he never talked too much, so I didn't know when things were right or when things were bad, but that's when he beat up, or tried to beat up on her, and that's when we knew that things weren't going right for him, you know. [What did you do during those times?] Well, as a youngster, I couldn't do too much, because my dad was a big man. [So you just walked out of the house?] Well, we had to sleep outside of the house, and, you know, stay away from him as much as possible.

This younger woman's parents had been divorced, and the violence occurred when the estranged father tried to come back: "He would usually come in the middle of the night because he was drunk and because he wanted to spend that time with us. My mom would throw him out and he would push her out of the way so he could enter the house. And that's when the fight would start. We would all jump in. We would pull them apart. It was like a nightmare all the time."

How did these people react when they saw their fathers beat their mothers? The two people just quoted represent the range: Almost two-thirds of the men and about half of the women withdrew in fear. More of the women (54 percent) tried to intervene, either to stop the battery or to fight the father themselves.

Much of the paternal violence—toward the kids as well as toward the mothers—appears to have been associated with heavy drinking. In more than 40 percent of these homes there was somebody that the respondent defined as an "alcoholic"—most often the father. The definition, of course, is not clinical, but seems to refer to a persistent pattern of heavy drinking, especially on weekends. The man just quoted describes his father's behavior when drunk and when sober:

> Whenever he got drunk, which was, uh, you know, at least once a week, he was totally two persons, you know, one when he was sober and another person when he was drinking, you know. [In other words when he was sober, he would just let things ride?] Yeah, yeah. [And when he drank, it came back to him and he thought he had something to say?] Yeah, or he would say it, or he'd have the—not the energy, but the guts, like the guts, *pues,* you know, the drinking would give him the power. That's when he became the mean bad wolf in the house, you know. . . . As a youngster I was very afraid of him, you know. He used to get real drunk and he would try to take it out on whoever was home, and usually I was at home as a youngster.

Relations with Parents

Whatever the source of paternal violence, more than half of these gang members were clearly afraid of their fathers when they were kids. For the boys, it was those in the earlier cliques, with more traditional parents, who were more likely to be afraid (66 percent as compared with 53 percent of the men from recent cliques). For the girls, women from earlier cliques were *less* likely to be afraid of their fathers (28 percent as compared with 68 percent of the women from more recent cliques).

Often there was good reason for fear: These were anything but ideal children. A man from an earlier clique and a man from a recent clique both describe much the same pattern. A third man from a recent clique experienced rather a bizarre punishment pattern.

[Were you ever afraid of your father?] Oh yes, because anything that he had in his hand, you know where it went—straight at me. Oh yes, I was scared of that man.

You know they used to really lay it on the line, you know what I mean. He says, "Hey, you blow it, you got to deal with me," you know what I mean. And take it to the fullest extent, you know. Ah man, one day I just took some money from him, and boy, man! And I smoked a cigarette, and ah, man, he made me smoke the whole carton, and it made me sick. He used to use an extension cord. He'd hit us with the closest thing to him. Whatever he could get his hands on. Extension cords, we had extension cords all over the house.

I'd either be spanked or hit with one of those—what do you call them, mimbrino branches? [A switch?] Yeah. I'd be spanked and tied. [Spanked and tied?] They would put a chain on me. [Is that right?] Yeah. Outside in the driveway. They used to tie me up with a chain, to a tree. [How long would they keep you tied up?] Oh, an hour or two.

Mothers were almost as fear-inspiring. Girls were more likely to be afraid of their mothers than were boys (55 percent as compared with 42 percent). Even though many men said that they were afraid of their mothers, they expressed more ambivalence than fear about their mothers. A man from an earlier clique recalled his Mexican-born mother: "I was afraid of my mother. I had more respect for her in a way. I would say, uh, I didn't want to hurt her, but when I hurt—when I knew that I hurt her, I was afraid of her in a sense that I knew she was angry and that hurt me, and that made me afraid of her." Girls were often in real fear of physical violence, like this woman from an earlier clique: "She would hit me, pinch me, and pull my hair, and then she'd have my brother— the oldest one—get a whip, and whip me, and then I'd have stripes all over my body like a zebra, and then I went to school like that." A younger woman, age 26 at the time of the interview, reflected on her violent relationship with her mother, which was still unresolved when she was interviewed:

Yeah, I was afraid. Because she used to beat me. But not no more.
When I was 16 I got her, and I got her on the floor and I pulled her
down and I cussed her and I said you never hit me again as long as
I live. Never. And to this day she'll never raise a hand to me. . . .
She would call me a whore, all kinds of bad names. I was gonna sleep
with men early. I was gonna get pregnant early. I was gonna work in
a potato factory. I was gonna have my house dirty. I told her, "Yeah,
come and see my house now!"

And another young woman had an even worse experience:

Yeah, she used to spank a lot, and then it got to where after a while
she wasn't spanking, she was hitting, and I was just afraid of her. [?]
Yeah, with the fist, and at times she threw things at me. One day she
threw a Sparkletts water bottle and one time she hit me in the eye
with it, or on the top of my head with a wine bottle, and it cracked my
head open. Just various things like that. Even got to a point where
at the age of 12 years old I tried to commit suicide because of the
problems my mother was giving me.

Girls were generally much more restricted than boys—especially
girls in the earlier cliques. We asked whether parents had been "strict or
easy" and whether they really enforced the rules or "just let things ride."
About 60 percent of the men said their parents were strict, and more than
80 percent said that they really did enforce the rules. Men from earlier
cliques were no more likely than ones from more recent cliques to say
that their parents had been strict. But 94 percent of the older women,
and 72 percent of the younger ones said that their parents were strict,
and almost all of the older women (though only half of the younger ones)
said that their parents really enforced the rules. The limitations placed
on girls sound like a litany of traditionalism, of parents trying to keep
their daughters from being "bad" girls (compare the "good girl–bad girl"
syndrome, described in Williams, 1989). For example, the young woman
just quoted talks about her father's attitude: "I couldn't even wear shorts.
I always had to be covered up, because he would just start calling us—
me and my sisters—that we were tramps. [How old were you then?]
OK, you know, when I started developing—I was about 12, until I was
23. He never stopped until the day he died." A woman from an earlier
clique recalled: "I could hardly go out. Cause when I went out I had to go

with my brother. He had to take me or else I couldn't go anywhere. Then after we'd get to the dance we'd separate and then we'd get together and come home. I wouldn't be able to get out of the house. Period."

These kinds of restrictions were common among families of the younger women as well. One young woman came from a cholo family; her mother and stepfather were both heroin addicts, but they continued to impose traditional norms on their daughter: "I couldn't have a boyfriend, you know. I had to come home early, straight from school, cook, and you know. [Did they really enforce the rules?] Yeah, yes. We'd get ready for school and my mother and stepfather would say 'You better come straight home from school.' We couldn't watch TV; we couldn't go out with nobody." Recall that these women were teenagers in the 1970s. Here is another one. "I was about, let's see, about 15, 14, around there. I was always—I couldn't—they wouldn't let me go out. I mean I couldn't go to the store by myself, that's how strict they were. So I'd tell my mom I'm going to the store, just to the store and back, and she would make me take one of my brothers with me." Sometimes parental strictness escalated, in futile reaction to the girls' adventures on the streets with the gang boys, as this older woman described: "I got pregnant and she got stricter, beat me up. She called my brother to beat me up. He didn't know why he was hitting me, though, until after. He asked her and she said because I was pregnant. I was only 14. I've been on my own since I was 14. I had two kids by the age of 15."

A number of men reported a pattern of increased tolerance as they moved into adolescence. "Boys will be boys" seems to have been the attitude. This man from a recent clique was raised by his mother and his grandparents: "Ah, they let things ride. When I started ditching, getting drunk at maybe 12 or 13 they thought it was part of growing up. They didn't feel that by restricting me that I was gonna stop. My grandfather had been through that too with his son. [How about your mother?] Oh, she would hit me or ground me, but she couldn't control me. I was too wild for her to control me." A man from an earlier clique reflects the same kind of age-related pattern: "OK let's go back to when I was younger. We couldn't step out of the front yard. Ever since I can remember to the age of 9 years old, there's no way that we could go out that we weren't restricted. . . . Up until the age that I was about 13, and then everything went wrong [laugh]. Everything. No more paying attention; I'd get whipped [laugh]."

Incest

People who study or treat women drug addicts often speculate that their drug use might be a means of coping with the long-range psychological traumas of incest. It also seems plausible that if family problems in general drive children to increased reliance on their friends and on the gang, incest would be the most extreme family problem for girls. Accordingly, we asked our respondents, "Did anybody in your family ever make any sexual advances to you when you were growing up?"

Twenty-nine percent of the women reported that some member of the family did so. This figure does not differ too much from estimates of incestuous experiences in the society in general. Our interviewers reported that there were a fair number of respondents who answered the question "no," but who hesitated enough before they answered to give the impression that they were not telling the truth. Thus this 29 percent probably understates the actual occurrence of incest in this sample. (Three men also reported sexual advances, but none seemed to treat the incident as a problem.)

As one would expect from the greater traditionalism of families in the earlier cliques, incest was more common in the older women's families than in the younger women's (39 percent compared with 24 percent of the younger women), even though the difference is not statistically significant. However, incest was not more common in homes with Mexican-born or poorly educated fathers.

Incest is generally associated with patriarchy, and there are indications that the more patriarchal homes were in fact more likely to be incestuous. Fathers of incest victims were more likely to beat their wives, and they were more likely to be strict with and depreciatory of their daughters. Incest victims were also more likely to see their fathers as alcoholics, but they were not significantly more likely to feel that their fathers were trying to set themselves up unequivocally as heads of the household or to control their mothers' visitors—other indicators of patriarchy.

In most cases the assailant was the father, but uncles, brothers, and grandfathers were among the culprits. And the experiences occurred at all ages, ranging from 5 to 17, with a median age of about 11½. In about 40 percent of the cases, only one approach was made, but the remainder reported repeated sexual encounters. There were comparatively few

long-term incestuous relationships like the ones described by these two
women from earlier cliques, one of whom makes explicit reference to the
gang as a refuge from an intolerable home situation:

> Yeah, my brother. I was 14 at the time, I think. [How long did it go
> on?] Ah, it went on a year, I think. And I didn't want—ah, I couldn't
> tell—ah, there was nobody to tell. My mother was never there and
> my father was always drunk. My sister had gotten married and left,
> and my other brother was too small. [?] He was 15. [?] Well, I would
> be asleep, and they would all get up and leave, you know, and like I
> was ditching school, and all that, you know. He would come and I'd
> wake up—and someone was staring at me, and it was him, over me
> on the couch, you know. And so, he'd attack me, you know, and I'd
> try to fight him, and, ah, the second time he did it I just—that's why
> I used to go to White Fence, see, and stay all the time.
>
> My grandfather, you know the things he did. He molested me. My
> dad, too. [Your dad, too, and he left you at a young age! How old
> were you when all this started?] I was like 7, or 6, and then with
> my dad I was like 9. . . . I had to keep all that to myself, you know,
> because I couldn't tell my grandma because that would hurt her, you
> know, so, ah, and I couldn't tell my father because he was doing the
> same thing, and then who could I tell, right? And then my, ah, my
> father's brother, too. I would sleep with my aunts. He would come
> to me when my aunts were asleep. And I don't know how he would
> wake me up, and he'd go like that, and I was afraid of him, right, and
> so I would have to go to him, you know, and he went all the way,
> too. . . . [How long did it go on with your grandfather?] Around four
> or five years. [And your dad?] About two years. [And the only times
> was when your father would babysit you? And your uncle only when
> he would come around?] Well, he lived there too, for a while. Ah, I
> think that went on for around a year and a half.

In both of these cases, the girl ultimately left the abusive home: the first
girl ran away to live with her uncle and aunt and returned home only after
her brother had been institutionalized, and the second girl went to live
with her mother. Both households were highly traditional: the first girl,
for example, was one of seventeen children, and the second girl's grand-

parents were very "Mexican." However, a note of family deviancy also enters: The second girl's father had been a gang member. Deviancy was specifically adduced by another woman in order to explain her father's behavior:

> Yeah, my father. When he came out of the joint. He must have been in his 40s. Well he went in when he was 28 and came out after 11 years. I was 12 then. It happened twice. [?] Dirty, I felt very dirty. [?] My mother at that time was sick and dying, and I couldn't tell my sisters, and I couldn't tell my brother. I couldn't tell nobody. [And it happened when he came out of the joint?] Yeah. [He was locked up so much—] Yeah, that's what I clean it up with too, that he done a lot of years, and he had just come out, and I was young, but I developed very early.

In a majority of cases, the girl told nobody about the approach and received no help. In a couple of instances, interviewers were the first to hear the story. Several women, like this older woman, mentioned the gang as a major source of support, and several fought back:

> [Did anybody in your family ever make sexual advances to you when you were growing up?] No, not in the family, but yes, my brother-in-law. [?] I was turning 11. He didn't get away with it though. [Did anybody help you with it?] No, I kept it all to myself, yeah, and he tried again when I was working, and I put him in his righteous place. I told him, "You better cool it, because I'm gonna get after you." Which was me and my friends from the barrio. See I used to turn to my friends in the barrio [i.e., the gang], you know, for help a lot of times because I couldn't get it at home, you know.

Girls who effectively resisted were often those who had been approached by someone other than their fathers, like this older woman:

> I was 12 or maybe 13. [Who was that, your stepfather?] Yes. See I would feel that the covers would be coming off me and I thought I was dreaming, but once I caught him doing it to me. And another time was that I was going to take a bath and we had like wooden floors and I happened to look down and I seen a hole and an eye looking up, so I went to tell my mother and she went and threw water so he came up all wet. But I was like a tomboy, and I wouldn't let myself—or else if

I would have been another type I would have been seduced. [So he never got—] No.

Running Away

Not surprisingly, given the restrictions placed on girls in general and the high incidence of incest, girls were notably more likely to have run away from home than boys. Almost a third of the boys ran away at least once, and boys from recent cliques were significantly more likely to have done so (38 percent compared with 20 percent of the boys from earlier cliques). By contrast, three-quarters of the girls ran away at least once, with no significant difference between girls from earlier and more recent cliques.

Sometimes the runaway incident was specifically related to incest. The girl just quoted, for example, ran away twice: "First time I was 16. I couldn't take it any more. My stepfather was getting to me. One time he tried to do something and I told him something so he got the belt and hit me and left me all marked up. So I had to get out of there." Other women ran from family assaults. This woman from an earlier clique found that running away was the only way that she could communicate with her mother:

> I was about 13. I ran away because my brother—my older brother—used to come home drunk and he used to try and hit me all the time. And my mother wasn't there, and I had to jump out the window and go hide down my girlfriend's house. So I got tired, tired, and when I got a little older I just ran away, just stood down Timber's house [homegirl]. And then I'd tell my little brother where I was, and I'd tell him, "Don't tell my mother cause I'm gonna let her get scared, so when she gets scared that something happened to me then she'll do something about it." I'd tell her and I'd tell her and she wouldn't do nothing, so I ran away for two weeks, and then my mom was really scared and she did something about it. Otherwise I couldn't get nothing done.

A slight majority (58 percent) of the girls who ran away did so only once, but many did so repeatedly. A younger woman clearly preferred living on the streets to living at home:

First time I was 10. At that time I wasn't very—my family wasn't a very happy family, so I found happiness out in the streets more. They were sharing that free love, and all that. So I went out to get some. It was the fighting at home, I guess, that they used to have. They were always fighting. I felt I didn't want that because I wasn't part of it. From the age of 10 on I was running away. Till I married at 15. Usually when they would find me I would be getting busted for something or getting loaded somewhere so I'd end up in juvenile hall.

And another younger woman, who ran away a total of five times, explained: "I seen my mom. I seen what she was doing. She was always using [heroin], and there was always no food in the house, and they were constantly fighting, and everything, you know."

In several cases, girls could better to be said to have left home than to have run away.

I was 13. I couldn't take it no more, I just couldn't get along with my dad. [How long did you stay away?] When I ran away I only ran away two blocks, and I stayed two years. [?] Well, I lived with my aunt for two years. From there I moved with my mom because she wasn't living with my dad. She was already separated.

I ran away [from an abusive mother] when I was 12 until I was about 15 years old. [?] I never went back home with my mother, no. After I was 12 I ran away to my older sister's house, and she got guardianship of me. She was just wonderful to me. She just took the mother role.

Other Family Problems

Some researchers (see Werner, 1983) suggest that stress is generated in a family when a member's problems begin to be a burden to the rest of the family. These families show a rather high incidence of such problems. I have mentioned "alcoholism." In addition, in a quarter of the men's homes and in 46 percent of the women's homes somebody was physically handicapped or chronically ill. Most often this was a parent. In 47 percent of the men's homes and 69 percent of the women's homes, some member died when the respondent was growing up. Most often this was a grandparent (in a third of the cases) but quite often it was a parent (a father in 30 percent of the homes and a mother in 11 percent) or a sibling (in 26 percent of the homes).

In addition to these traumas, which tended to involve older members of the household, siblings' deviance also generated family strains. Thus 20 percent of the men and 45 percent of the women grew up with a heroin addict in the home—most often a brother. And, finally, 57 percent of the men and 82 percent of the women saw somebody in their homes arrested when they were children. In 56 percent of these homes, it was a brother that was arrested. (The gender differences reflect the fact that gang girls were more likely than boys to have a gang-member brother at home.) In 28 percent of the homes, it was the respondent's father; these tended to be the cholo families. In 17 percent of the cases, respondents reported their own arrests during early adolescence. Even though most of these families seem reasonably conventional and hard-working, there seem to be a large number of families with troubles.

There are a couple of inferences that can be drawn from these rather dry statistics.

First, it is important to note that there are no statistically significant differences between earlier and more recent cliques in the incidence of these problems. We might have expected families in more recent times to have more problems, but that is clearly not the case.

The second point is that *clearly* more women than men came from troubled families. They were more likely to have been living with a chronically sick relative, one who died, one who was a heroin addict, or one who was arrested. In fact, a large majority of the women had a relative die or be arrested. This seems on the face of it to imply that the gang represents a different kind of peer-group outlet to its female members than to its male members, and that for girls it may in fact be more of a refuge from family problems, as some of the women quoted earlier say.

Conclusions

This review of family functioning has been guided by a literature that calls for a search for problems. In addition, we have tried to find whether problems might be greater or lesser among more recent gang cliques.

There is no doubt that we found problems, sometimes severe, in many of these families. But the findings do not cast much light on the broader question about how family problems affect gang membership.

For example, we have no way of telling whether these families had more problems than their neighbors in the barrios. Further, the search for problems may itself be misleading: it assumes that there are just two kinds of families—good and bad. Most families, of course, are a mixture of the two. Thus many of our respondents were reared in highly conventional families in which they were the "black sheep," like this man from one of the recent cliques, who was asked how his folks reacted to the gang: "Negative because my family's never been in a gang. I'm the black sheep of my family. There aren't any relatives that are gang members. All my relatives are pretty successful in my family. They're always workers and never criminals." This was a "good" family that could not control one of its members. On the other extreme, there were clearly some "bad" families: Some were riddled with abusiveness; a few were headed by parents who themselves were cholos, and unable to order their own lives, let alone those of their children (see Chapter Seven on "inheritance" of gang membership).

But what do we say about those in-between, mixed families? Striking a balance is difficult. Maladaptive parenting may affect one sibling more than another. Thus an incestuous father may deeply damage a girl—and send her directly to the gang—while her brother may emerge unscathed. And an overburdened parent may rear his or her first few children with effective controls but just "give up," as some of our respondents said, on the youngest children in the family. Some female-headed households may be extremely effective in controlling their children, while others, in essence, simply collapse (see Moore and Vigil, 1987, for a typology of families).[5]

Nor is there any easy answer about an increase or decrease in family problems. Some problems—notably those that theory tells us might be associated with traditionalism and patriarchy—have declined. Thus fewer of the younger men were afraid of their fathers, and fewer of the younger women were incest victims. But other problems—those that might be associated with choloization—were more frequent among families of more recent clique members: There were more female-headed households among the recent clique members, there was more spousal battery, and the men (but not women) were more likely to have run away from home. And, allowing for a bit of anachronism, Thrasher's (1927) worries about immigrant families gain some support from these data. But again, one must be cautious. Girls were particularly likely to chafe under the pressures of traditional role restrictions, for example, but this was almost as common among Los Angeles–born parents, acting in the 1970s, as among the Mexican-born parents acting in the 1950s.

Perhaps the most significant finding is that there are so few differences between families in earlier and more recent cliques—apart from the obvious and expected differences in immigrant status, that is. There *were* problems in many of these families, but any notion that the passing generations either diminished or exacerbated such problems is generally not borne out by the data. Perhaps the strongest lesson is that then, as now, gang members come from troubled families.

chapter seven

Growing Up

Most researchers on gangs emphasize the adolescent years. But what happens after adolescence when gang members grow up? People often assume that once a kid joins a gang he or she is doomed to street life, interspersed with periods in prison. Our own previous work has looked at adults who were in gangs, but even that work might well confirm such an assumption because we were limited to interviewing heroin addicts and ex-prisoners who happened to have been members of gangs (Moore et al., 1978; Moore with Devitt, 1989).

By contrast, in this study a random sample of *all* of the gang members was interviewed, not just those who obviously wound up on the bottom. For the first time we can say something about what happened to gang members in general as they moved into adulthood, and not just about the losers. This reflects the gang as a quasi-institution in the barrios. The degree of street involvement of former gang members still may be overstated simply because some of the more respectable men and women declined to be interviewed. (I describe this in the Appendix.) However, it is a much better position than if we just looked at addicts and convicts. I will deal first with the problems—drugs and prison—and then address more general questions about the family life of these men and women and how they were making a living.

Addicts and Nonaddicts: Drugs and Prison

Tecatos

In the late 1980s, cocaine and crack were publicized as the drug plague of poor communities. However, Chicanos had been faithful to heroin ever since its introduction in the 1950s and they have continued to focus on the drug even into the late 1980s. In fact, in the Southwest there was a little-publicized but serious heroin epidemic in the 1980s, with heroin-related deaths escalating dramatically during the decade (Crider, Groerer, and Blanken, 1989). And, not surprisingly, heroin continued to be by far the most serious drug for our respondents.

The *tecato* life-style has been portrayed in several accounts (e.g., Casavantes, 1976; Jorquez, 1984), but it may help to give condensed life histories of one man from an early clique and one woman from a more recent clique. The man was 50 years old when he was interviewed. His parents moved to El Hoyo Maravilla when he was a baby, and he continued to live there—with his family—all his life. He joined the gang when he was 15 and began using heroin when he was 16, just chipping a couple of days a week, making money to score by doing odd jobs, and "stealing and dealing." He went to jail (Youth Authority) that same year, on a heroin-related charge, served a year, and came back to the barrio, where he rejoined his homies and began to use heroin more frequently. He began selling narcotics again, and went back to jail for another year. When he was released, he again began a heroin run, and though he no longer dealt heroin, for several years he began a pattern of doing County jail time—three or four months to a year—for "marks."[1] The pattern was interrupted at the age of 23, when he went to prison, was resumed when he came out three years later, and was interrupted again when he went to prison from the ages of 28 to 30 and again from the ages of 32 to 36. Every time he was released he went back to his heroin using friends. But then he "stopped doing time." He never held a job until he was almost 40, when he worked a year for the County, as a custodian. His heroin use tapered off: he was "just chipping." He quit altogether when he was in his early 40s. He survived by doing odd jobs—gardening, painting. He lived with a woman, briefly, when he was 19, and fathered a daughter, but saw very little of her. Major turning points: In his teens? "Using drugs." In his 20s? "I started going to jail." In his 30s? "Just that I went to prison." In his 40s? "By staying out of jails and prison." His summary: "I wasted most of my life, behind them prisons, jails, kicking habits."

Very few of the women in the earlier cliques used heroin. A woman from a recent White Fence clique, born in 1960, exemplifies many women users: Her father was a conventional, home-owning, working man until he was injured when she was 13 and the family became dependent on welfare. She was one of 13 siblings; several of her brothers were gang members and one was dealing marijuana when she was a teenager. One was a heroin addict, and was "in and out, in and out" of prison, and one brother died of an overdose of heroin. She joined the gang when she was 14, was arrested on a felony charge, but only served three months' time. She had her first child when she was 17, and also started using heroin at the same time—with her boyfriend (who was not a gang member). The relationship didn't last long, but he continued to supply her with heroin even after they broke up. She had two more children with another boyfriend, moved out of her parents' house and continued to use heroin, going on a long run for four years up to and including the time she was interviewed. She was never imprisoned, even though she and her current boyfriend were dealing heroin. She held a job only once, when she was still a teenager, just before she dropped out of school. The major turning point in her teens was the birth of her daughter, and in her twenties: "Drugs. That changed everything." Her life-style began to revolve around the need to get money for heroin.

When did the tecatos start using heroin? Except for a handful of experimenters, most of the gang members who used heroin did not start until their late teens, usually in the gang context. Even then, it was primarily men, not women, who used heroin. (Almost half of the men, but less than a quarter of the women were using heroin by the age of 20). But, as Long (1990) argues, by the age of 20, "many of these individuals had been labeled tecatos—heroin addicts" even within the gang. They tended to withdraw into their own subcliques even if they remained active in the gang.

It wasn't *just* labeling: those who became seriously involved with the drug became preoccupied with the hustling life-style that heroin use dictates. This was a major life change. We asked, "What do you think were the major changes in your life, the times when your life really saw a change, like when you were in your teens?" A full 39 percent of all of the men and 16 percent of the women named "heroin, drugs, narcotics" as the major happening of their teens. No matter how much heroin they were actually using during their teens, these men and women were acknowledging the fact that it was during their teens that they were initiated into the world of heroin and its usually disastrous life consequences.

One man who started heroin when he was 17 said, "The clock stopped for me then." Street life preoccupied him almost continuously for years to come.

Even though this chapter focuses on the adult years, it is almost essential to raise a few background questions about the tecatos. Did they come from different kinds of families than the majority of gang members who did not get involved with heroin? We find there are astonishingly few differences. Among the men, tecatos were no more likely than nonusers to come from abusive families, or particularly poverty-stricken families, or families that had an alcoholic or an addict. Women heroin users *were* more likely to have had a father who beat his wife than were nonusers (48 percent compared with 24 percent) but, contrary to much speculation, they were *not* more likely to have been victims of incest. They were notably more likely to have grown up with an addict in the home—often a brother (60 percent of the users as compared with 34 percent of the nonusers).

Nor were there many differences in gang experiences: tecatos and tecatas did not join the gang at earlier ages; they were not more likely to have confined their social and dating relations to other gang members; nor were they more likely to feel that the gang was "very important." They were not more likely to have considered themselves as muy loco; nor were their parents more likely to have been permissive about their gang involvement.

One thing did distinguish heroin users from nonusers when it comes to the gang: they were significantly more likely to answer the question "Are you all for your barrio now?" with a resounding "Yes." Obviously, the difference lies in the fact that the tecatos were still relying on their homeboys both on the streets and in prison. For some, like this 52-year-old tecato, such reliance was a total way of life: "The barrio, you get away from the barrio it's different, you know. It'd be different because, you know, when you're away from your barrio you're not comfortable. I got to be in my barrio to feel comfortable, good. But if I go out of my barrio I don't feel right, you know."

Sex Differences

These two brief life histories capture some characteristic differences between men and women tecatos. Men tend to start heroin and to continue the life-style largely within the peer group. Men were also much more likely to go to prison, and to spend their lives "in and out, in and out." Women tended to be preoccupied with their children, even when they didn't stay with their husbands or rear their children (see Moore with Devitt, 1989), while men tended to lose contact with their children when they left their wives. It was rare, but by no means unknown, for tecatos of either sex to be fully involved in the world of work.

By contrast, as indicated above, women were more likely to grow up in a household with an addicted brother or father. Women were also much more likely to have their heroin use bracketed by a mate: They tended to start heroin use with a boyfriend or husband, and, even though each liaison might be short-lived, the street world almost dictates that a tecata's next boyfriend will also be a heroin user. To some extent, then, women's heroin use is enacted in a familial context. It might be seen as a twisted version of the usual Mexican emphasis on family roles for women. (See also Moore with Devitt, 1989, and Moore, 1990, for an analysis of family background among Chicana addicts.)

For both men and women heroin users, it is not much of an exaggeration to say that heroin ruined their lives, but in different ways.

Methadone: Not a Panacea for Heroin

In the late 1960s, the synthetic opiate methadone was highly touted as a panacea for heroin addicts: combined with counseling, it offered the hope for rehabilitation. However, as is usual with drug programs for the poor, methadone was never combined with effective counseling in East Los Angeles, and it certainly never became a panacea for addiction.

As our sample moved from their 20s to their 30s and 40s and wanted to quit the heroin life-style, increased proportions enrolled in methadone programs. But at the peak, when men and women were in their early 40s, only 11 percent of the sample were in methadone programs while 32 percent were still using heroin. Women tended to be enrolled in methadone programs more frequently than men, but still at low levels compared to the proportions using heroin. These figures should not obscure the fact that for the handful of men and women enrolled in the programs, methadone provided a means for staying clean and continuing to work. Even if still another dependency, it was a lifeline to some degree of normalcy. But such people were exceptions.

What went wrong with the glorious idea? A lot of things. To begin with, methadone rapidly acquired a reputation among addicts for generating serious health problems: stomach problems, impotency, and obesity (for women) were reported (see Beschner and Walters, 1985). In addition, ironically, it was much more difficult and painful to get *off* methadone (to detox) than from heroin. Obviously, these and other experiences deterred a certain number of addicts, as did the high cost: At the time we interviewed, methadone cost $130 a month—an extraordinarily high proportion of the monthly check for a man or woman on welfare.

"Who needed it?" was a common reaction, especially since, for many men and women who combined methadone with boozing, it was just another chemical dependency. In addition, the methadone programs in East Los Angeles had bad reputations among the addicts: The parking lots were easy spots for dealing pills, heroin, and even methadone. (A few addicts who could take their methadone home with them consumed just enough to keep them from getting sick and sold the rest to people who had been expelled from methadone programs or who wanted to kick their heroin habit without entering the programs.) Fights were common, and killings were not unknown. And staff people in several programs were suspected of diluting the dosages and selling the methadone on their own.

Finally, methadone had simply become a part of the tecato life-style. It was used by many as an occasional expedient to come down from an excessively expensive heroin habit. Clearly, methadone had its place, and an important one. But it was not a panacea.

Addiction and Arrests in Respondents' Households

The tecato life-style may last throughout the addict's life, or it may be short-term. At the time they were interviewed, 24 percent of the men were addicted. In addition, a few of these addicts were married to addicted women or had an addicted son or daughter living with them. Thirty-two percent of the women were addicted; 21 percent were living with an addicted spouse, and a few had addicted children or brothers in the households.

These figures once again illustrate the greater vulnerability of women gang members to long-range problems. In their teens, half of the men were using heroin, but by the time of the interview only 24 percent were doing so. In their teens, a quarter of the women were using heroin, but by the time of the interview 43 percent were involved in some way in the heroin life-style, either addicted themselves or living with an addict.

The figures on arrest patterns are also very telling. Arrests are often heroin-related, of course. When we asked if any member of the household had ever been arrested, 49 percent of the men and 33 percent of the women responded affirmatively. All of the men referred to themselves: They all had been arrested. By contrast, only half of these women had been arrested. In almost all cases, it was their husbands who had been arrested.

These data all add up to the fact that heroin is important, so important that in the remainder of this chapter I report differences between the behavior of those respondents who used heroin as well as differences between respondents from earlier and more recent cliques of the gang. The measure is heroin use during the teens: Most of the respondents who used heroin in their teens (90 percent of the men and all of the women) continued to do so into their twenties.

Family Life

Marriages

Most of these men and women—addicts and nonaddicts alike—had been married at least once (87 percent of the men and 96 percent of the women). But at the time of the interview, married life was not the norm. Among the men, only a third of the men from recent cliques were living with a wife. Slightly more than half of the men from earlier cliques were living with a wife. Among the women, 45 percent of the women from recent cliques but only a third of the women from the earlier cliques were living with a husband.

Basically, marriages did not last. This was particularly true for the men who used heroin early in their lives. Most of these men began to go in and out of prison when they were in their teens, and if they did marry or live with a woman, the first serious spell in prison usually terminated the relationship. As an illustration, one man was 29 when he was interviewed. When he was 15, he was serving the third of a series of short-term sentences. He ran away from the camp, and instead of going home he set himself up in an independent apartment. He made a substantial profit on one major theft, and put it into heroin. He started to live with his girlfriend from the gang. She had a baby, and he found a job—continuing to deal heroin—and they lived together for almost a year. A year or so later, he got married to another girl. That marriage lasted a couple of years until he went back to jail again for four years. When he got out, he moved in with his parents and began using heroin heavily, going in and out of prison. Whenever he was out, he lived with his parents. He describes his family life:

> I never lived with nobody else but my wife. I mean, I have broads I sleep with, but they're not, you know, it's just girlfriends, you know what I mean. We don't live together or nothing. [Who raised your kids?] Which ones? OK, I have two kids but they're from different broads, you know what I mean. One's from my wife and one's from this girl I knew when I was young, so their mothers raised them. I never raised none of them.

Like this man, most heroin users started living with a mate at earlier ages than gang members who avoided the drug life-style. (Twenty percent of the heroin-using men and 42 percent of the heroin-using women were living with someone at age 16 or younger, compared with 7 percent of the nonusing men and 8 percent of the nonusing women.)

Even the men and women who avoided heroin tended to have been divorced or separated—often more than once. This is not because they married especially early, since the median age at marriage was not dramatically lower for these men and women than for other Americans.[2] One source of difficulty is that many of the more conventional men continued to hang around with their homeboys, even after marriage. For example, one man, born in 1932, never used heroin and lived a reasonably conventional life, finally buying his own barbershop. He married his girlfriend from the gang when he got out of the Korean war at the age of 21: "I got married but I still used to go down to the barrio to drink booze and smoke weed with Genero and Joker, my friends from the barrio. It was just weekends and special occasions: I worked most of the time." This man had been married formally once, and twice lived for long periods of time in common-law marriages. It wasn't until he was into his 40s that he gave up hanging around with his homeboys.

Hanging around with the homeboys, down in the barrio—if only on weekends—often leads to problems for the family. First of all it means that the emotional focus remains strongly on the gang. This weakens marriages. Second, a number of respondents, especially men, described times when their marriages were in crisis and the lure of the street lifestyle reasserted itself. They often describe bouts of heavy drinking or reimmersion in drugs, or, as with this same man, a brief fling with illicit activity:

[How about at 39 years old, you did another year in jail. For what?] Sale of heroin. [At what age did you start dealing?] I wasn't actually dealing then. The last time I got caught, though, I was. That was in 1971 for sale of heroin. I just did it because I was separated from my ex-wife. I was in the county jail. That was the last time I got into any problems. I tried to just change my life. At that time I just said, 'That's it.' Kinda late, though, but. . . .

Another gang-related source of marital instability that is especially important for women is the tendency to marry other gang members. Slightly more than a third of the men, but 55 percent of the women had been married to a gang member. (The practice was especially common among those who used heroin as teenagers: half of the men, and two-thirds of the women heroin users had lived with a gang member, compared with only 16 percent of the nonusing men and 51 percent of the nonusing women.) These are often youthful marriages, and neither partner is really willing to give up involvement with the gang.

The importance of nongang as compared with gang spouses is underscored by a very square man, who married for the first and only time when he was 22: "You know what helped me a lot? My wife. I still wanted to get high and everything. But my wife. You know how they are when you first get married. They don't want you to be the same. And I married a pretty decent girl. She was pretty well off. More than we are. [And she kept you from getting in . . .]—trouble and all that."

To this picture of precarious marriage we should add an important point: Parents are usually the backstop, especially for men.

Having Children

Most of these men and women had children—82 percent of the men and 94 percent of the women. Men had fewer children than women (an average of 2.9 compared with 3.4), and adolescent heroin users had fewer children. (Nonusing men had an average of 2.9 children compared with 2.8 for users, and nonusing women had an average of 3.6 children compared with 2.7 children for users.)

Most of the women (85 percent) raised their children, but only a minority of the men (43 percent) did so. Adolescent heroin users—male and female alike—were significantly less likely to have raised their own children. Men left the children with their wives (the children's mothers), while women (36 percent of them) left some of them to their relatives. Elsewhere (Moore with Devitt, 1989) we have analyzed this pattern among Chicana heroin users. Our data indicated that addicted women from traditional families tend to leave their children with their parents, while women addicts from more cholo families tend to keep their children, even during periods of active heroin use.

Having children is a major turning point for many women. Forty-three percent of the women, but only 19 percent of the men listed parenthood as a major turning point in their teens and twenties. Later in the interview we asked whether the respondents now considered themselves as loco as when they were active in the gang. Women were more likely to explain their conversion to conventionality as a consequence of motherhood, as this interviewer commented: "I'm square now. [And when did the change come about?] When I had my first baby. [That's what everybody says—when they had their first kid—all the girls.] Yeah."

Among those respondents who did bring up their children, only a minority reported that they had problems doing so. More women reported that they had problems—and more serious problems. It is particularly interesting that women were more likely than men to report that their children had joined gangs (22 percent of the women compared with 5 percent of the men, with early heroin users no more likely to have children in a gang). This is not surprising. Male gang members were less likely than women to marry a gang member in the first place, and even less likely to live with their children. Thus most of the men's children were brought up by square mothers, whereas the "gang tradition," if there is such a thing, was more likely to be present in a woman's household. Media and police delight in the myth that East Los Angeles gangs are "hereditary," with membership passed on from father to son. This is obviously not the case. When we asked how they felt about their children's being in a gang, most responses were vehement: a 30-year-old woman mourned: "Yeah, they're very involved in a gang, my kids. [How do you feel about that?] Bad. I was in the joint when they started getting involved." And a 35-year-old man went further:

I don't want them to, you know. I'm totally against my kids getting involved in any barrio, you know. I don't want them to lead the life

I did, I lived. And I'm going to try to the best of my knowledge and ability to keep it that way, you know. Because I can use myself as an example towards them, you know, this is what happened when I did it, you know what I mean. If you don't believe me, hey you want to try it, you know, I'm telling you, you know what I mean. I know what's wrong, and what's right, and what are you going to get out of it if you take that road.

Survival Strategies at the Time of Interview

Generally, these men and women relied on jobs for their livelihoods. But, like many economically marginal people in the United States, they had other survival strategies as well. Let us first look at their success in the conventional labor markets.

Work

When these respondents were interviewed, there were significant differences between members of earlier and more recent cliques in their propensity to work. Sixty-one percent of the men and 44 percent of the women from the earlier cliques were working, as compared with only 48 percent of the men but 61 percent of the women from recent cliques. Men who had used heroin during their teens were significantly less likely to be working than men who had abstained. (The figures are 50 percent versus 64 percent.)

Work was the principal survival strategy of most of our respondents. Even though a fair number of respondents were unemployed at the time of interview, almost all of the men—from recent as well as earlier cliques— had worked within the preceding five-year period (85 percent), as had three-quarters of the women from recent cliques and 61 percent of the women from earlier cliques. Thirty percent of the men had been fired from their previous jobs, and almost a quarter had been laid off. Others had found a better job or opened a business, or quit in disgust, or had a variety of other problems (moves, arrests).

About a third of the working men (33 percent) and women (37 percent) were in semiskilled factory jobs, with no significant difference between members of earlier and more recent cliques. About a third (37 percent) of the working women but only a small fraction of the working men were unskilled workers. Men's jobs were considerably more diverse than women's, with a number of men holding skilled (18 percent) and semiprofessional jobs (12 percent). A full 21 percent were working only part time.

Neither women nor men earned much: The median was only $1,200 a month, with older men (but not women) earning higher incomes.[3] The highest paid quartile made more than $1,800 a month. These were people who had held their jobs for the longest period and included skilled and semiskilled workers as well as the few professionals and entrepreneurs.[4] The lowest paid quartile earned less than $799 a month. These men and women were more likely to be part-time workers.

Most of the people (60 percent of the men and 57 percent of the women) found their jobs through personal connections—friends, homies, and relatives, in that order. And though 36 percent of the men and 43 percent of the women were in union jobs, only 2 men and none of the women had been helped by the union to obtain a job.

Most respondents were reasonably satisfied with their jobs (especially the higher paid men), and the majority (especially the older and lower paid men) recognized that they would need more education or retraining to get a better job. While English fluency had been a job problem for only a handful, 19 percent of the men and 12 percent of the women had enough trouble with basic literacy skills to be handicapped in the job market. (All of these people had been educated the Los Angeles school system.) A third of the men and a quarter of the women—especially the most poorly paid—felt that they had been victims of job discrimination.

Looking at some other job-related issues, most were in reasonably good health, but 16 percent of the men and 10 percent of the women were physically handicapped and could not work. And, in a city in which public transportation is extraordinarily expensive and time-consuming, only 61 percent of the men and 51 percent of the women had a car in running order. Having a car was directly and strongly correlated with the rate of pay: The better paid were more likely both to have a car and a valid driver's license.

Other Survival Strategies

In addition to their own salaries, many respondents—especially women—depended on the salaries of other people in their households. In the vast majority of the households at least one person was working. Only

7 percent of the men lived in homes where no one worked, as did 3 percent of the younger women and 11 percent of the older women. About 40 percent of the women lived with a working husband, and about the same proportion of the women from earlier cliques lived with daughters or sons who worked. Men were less likely to have a working spouse (15 percent of the younger and 27 percent of the older respondents), but almost 20 percent lived with brothers or sisters who worked, and younger men also tended to have working parents or other working members of the household. This multiple income strategy is, of course, common among poor Hispanics in general.

In addition to one's own work and that of relatives, there are other sources of income. Almost a third of the men—younger as well as older—had received some form of government transfer payments within the preceding five-year period. These included welfare, disability, and SSI payments. Contrary to stereotype, women were much less likely to rely on such payments. Only 17 percent of the older women and 9 percent of younger women reported obtaining income from welfare, disability, or SSI. These figures are probably not much higher than those for other poor Mexican Americans (see Tienda and Jensen, 1988).

A quarter of the younger respondents—female as well as male—also reported some income from illicit activity. Eighteen percent of the older men and 11 percent of the older women also reported illicit income. Most of the income was from small-scale drug dealing or other "hustles," with a small minority (8 percent of the younger men and 3 percent of the younger women) reporting household income from burglary or other property crimes. Property crimes as a source of income was inconsequential among older respondents.

Work and Survival Strategies in Young Adulthood

In many respects, these contrasts between members of earlier and more recent cliques give a distorted picture. Older people generally tend to be more stable, both in jobs and marriages. We should, instead, look at the work and survival strategies of our respondents at comparable ages, the early and late 20s in particular. Times were different in the 1950s, and this is the point: The comparison can give some indication of how life has changed for gang members—a better indication than the contrast between jobs now held by younger and older members. We do not have much information on the *kinds* of jobs held, but we do have information on whether they were working.

Work

First, let us look at men's jobs. There were some surprises here. Men from recent cliques were almost as likely to have worked during their early 20s as were men from earlier cliques, and even more likely to have worked during their late 20s.[5] Thus the fact that significantly more of the men from recent cliques were unemployed at the time of the interview does not necessarily mean that they were out of the labor market.

Were they imprisoned? High proportions of the men—41 percent—reported that they spent some time in prison during their early 20s, but men from recent cliques were no more likely to have been in prison than men from earlier cliques. This really is not too surprising: The 1950s saw the first heavy waves of imprisonment as the criminal justice system began to crack down on heroin dealers. El Hoyo Maravilla, in particular, was a target for federal law enforcement, and a number of our respondents were caught.[6]

It looks, then, as if it might be something about the job situation itself rather than about changed characteristics of the gang or the men that accounts for higher rates of unemployment among men from recent cliques at the time of the interview. It is not that the men from recent cliques were more likely to have dropped out of the labor market, nor were they more likely to be imprisoned. It may be that they could not get full-time, stable jobs.

Among the women, there were no significant employment differences between members of earlier and of more recent cliques.[7] Men's jobs have tended to disappear or to be downgraded, but women's local job opportunities stayed pretty much the same—not very good, but not much changed. Imprisonment was unimportant for most women: Fewer than 6 percent went to prison during their 20s.

Other Survival Strategies

In their 20s, men and women from the earlier cliques tended to rely on income provided by other working members of the household as well as their own jobs, just like members of the recent cliques. In fact, they were *more* likely to do so. They were notably more likely to live with a working

Table 7-1.   Who Was Earning in the Household When Respondent Was Aged 20–29: By Sex and Earlier and Recent Cliques

Sex and Clique	Respondent	Spouse	Father	Mother	Sibling	Other	N
a. Ages 20–24							
Male							
Earlier Cliques	63.0%	6.5%	43.5%	13.0%	37.0%	6.5%	46
Recent Cliques	56.7	8.3	36.7	23.3	18.3	10.0	60
Female							
Earlier Cliques	55.6	38.9	50.0	22.2	33.3	16.7	18
Recent Cliques	54.5	42.4	15.2	33.3	18.2	6.0	33
b. Ages 25–29							
Male							
Earlier Cliques	65.2	8.7	34.8	10.9	30.4	0	46
Recent Cliques	73.3	11.7	18.3	11.7	6.7	6.6	60
Female							
Earlier Cliques	66.7	44.4	22.2	11.1	27.8	11.1	18
Recent Cliques	60.6	45.5	12.1	21.2	18.2	12.1	33

brother or sister, and also notably more likely to be living at home with working fathers (Table 7-1). Men from the recent cliques may have left home at earlier ages.

Income reported from transfer payments tended to be fairly low: even lower at comparable ages for respondents from earlier cliques. This may be because fewer programs were available and government programs were generally underutilized by the Mexican-American population in the 1950s and 1960s.

Men from the earlier cliques also relied on illicit income when they were in their 20s—though not quite as heavily as men from the recent cliques at the same ages (Table 7-2). But women from the earlier cliques did not—or at least did not report it to our interviewers. Though the number of women from early cliques is small, this pattern conforms to our expectations: Women in the earlier cliques tended to be kept out of criminal activities. The proportions reporting any illegal income declined rapidly after the mid-30s, for both men and women.

Table 7-2. Nonwage Income When Respondent Was
Aged 20–29: By Sex and Earlier and Recent Cliques

Sex and Clique	Illegal Income	Transfer Payments	N
a. Ages 20–24			
Male			
Earlier Cliques	34.8	10.9	46
Recent Cliques	50.0	16.7	60
Female			
Earlier Cliques	0	5.6	18
Recent Cliques	27.3	18.2	33
b. Ages 25–29			
Male			
Earlier Cliques	28.3	8.7	46
Recent Cliques	36.8	10.5	60
Female			
Earlier Cliques	0	0	18
Recent Cliques	29.0	16.1	33

Hangouts

If they are not working, what do these men and women do? Like all
unemployed people, many just hang around. But many of these men and
women continue to hang around with their homeboys and homegirls.
Earlier we suggested that this prolongs adolescence by perpetuating the
emotional focus on the gang. It also means that the man is vulnerable
on several counts. The barrio is the principal hangout of homeboys who
are involved in the heroin life-style, and the man may feel obligated to
give favors to such homeboys, like one Maravilla man who got in trouble:
"At 27 years old I was busted for possession of heroin. [Did you ever
use heroin?] No. I just happened to give this guy a ride downtown. We
were stopped by the police and he threw the heroin underneath the seat.
I was charged with transporting heroin. I spent almost a year in the

county jail fighting the case. I won the case but I lost my car." Hangouts
have changed over time. One member of the original White Fence clique
recalls that there were few hangouts when he was a young adult.

[When you were 20, 23 years old, did you have a job?] Yeah. Most
of us [from the clique] had work. . . . [When you got out of prison,
when you were 28, what were the guys doing?] Let's see, that was
1956. First I go find a job and most of the guys are working. Not
too many guys from my clique hanging around. . . . There were
not too many people you could go see. Because everybody was
working, at work, most of them. This was when I was coming out of
prison, right. Your own clique, your own age, had moved on. They
had gotten married: Huero was up north; Ferdinand wasn't out yet.
[These were all people in your clique?] Yeah. They were going to this
girl's house way out at the end of Wabash Road. It was a hangout for
guys and some of the girls. They were using there. It was primarily
a drug users' house. It was a take-off point to go hustle, or go steal,
or boost. I tried it: it didn't work out—I went out a couple of days,
right? I spent all day with these guys and didn't make two cents. . . .
I said I could make more money than this working, you know, and not
wind up so tired. [Were there other guys from your clique hanging
around each others' houses?] These were guys from outside my
clique. They were users; they needed a place to fix.

When this respondent came out of prison at the age of 28, he could
find only one hangout house to go to, and it never occurred to him to join
the younger cliques who were hanging out on the streets. By contrast, a
28-year-old leaving prison today has a dozen different places to go, both
in homes and on the streets, with people from different cliques present.
Some of them will be addicts, some will be hustlers or thieves, and some
are just hanging around, using whatever drugs they can find, or getting
in their cars to visit a hangout in another part of the neighborhood to vary
the scene.

Street hangouts collect the younger kids and some of the older men
who are still closely identified with the gang, but houses are more common among older men. A man from a recent White Fence clique, in his
mid-30s when interviewed, is wary of the visibility of street hangouts,
but his own home has become a hangout:

[How come I don't see you over there on Camulos?] Oh right there at Blueberry Hill? I used to hang around right there, but I hate to front myself, so . . . everybody's standing on the corner and the cops come around. They see you; they see your face; they get familiar with you. I'm trying to really get out of the limelight. Out of sight out of mind. . . . Every time I was over there I'd get harassed. [I don't understand them sitting right there on the corner, because to me it's asking for the cops to come and fuck you over or for somebody to come by and shoot at you.] These guys don't feel they're in any danger at all. They've been there for years. I used to go hang around there. That was quite some time ago. But I said "no more," because they popped caps on us quite a few times. A couple of youngsters got hit a couple of times. . . . [Do you still see any of the guys from your clique?] Every day. Maybe once or twice a day. They come down to my house. Like I live right in the barrio. We usually sit down in my backyard and have a few beers. That's way back where I live. Out of sight, out of mind. . . . Even guys from other barrios go down my pad. Vatos from Hoyo Mara, Vatos from Varrio Nuevo, King Kobras, you know. They're older dudes. They're not into the gang-banging thing. Most of the guys that go down my house are older, so we sit down and talk.

The increased number of young adults hanging around the streets with younger gang members may have had an effect on the gang social structure. A decade ago, each of the cliques in these two gangs was reasonably distinct and self-contained, and that was the model we used when we began our study. One of the cliques we sampled, however, was not like this. The structure of this clique reflect changes in hangout patterns hinted at above, and a general blurring of the age grading system. This in turn has implications for the gang as an agency of socialization.

First, this clique—the Monstros—was very large: while most cliques in both gangs ranged between 25 and 50 members, we identified 163 members in the Monstros. Second, the clique lasted a very long time. It departed from the normal pattern of age-graded recruiting. Normally, male cliques recruit new members during a few years of adolescence, and all members are within a few years of each other in age. Unlike all of the other cliques studied, the Monstros, formed in 1968, were still actively recruiting in 1985 from among teenagers in the neighborhood, as were the Monstras—their female counterpart. The oldest respondent from this clique was born in 1949 while the youngest was born in 1964—a very unusual age span. The youngest respondent was only four years old when the clique got started. Reputedly the members who were doing most of the recruiting were unemployed young men who were actively involved in drug use and petty dealing, and they were attracting younger men through drug networks. The drugs included PCP and heroin.

Some indication of the continuing involvement of older men is given in an interview with a 41-year-old White Fence man. Normally he hangs around with three or four men from his own clique, usually in the street hangout that attracts the kids—the one that our previous respondent avoids. He told an elaborate story about how he got involved with gang recruitment, actually helping to arrange the ritual jumping-in. Five kids from a community about ten miles away came to their uncle—his friend, who is 36 years old. The "kids" ranged in age from 14 to 20.

> I say, "How come you want to be in White Fence." He goes, *"Sabes que*, I want to be one of the boys." I tripped out on that one. I say, "I'm sure there's something; you must of did somebody wrong. How come you come all the way here to get into the barrio?" He goes, "My uncle's from White Fence and if I'm gonna be in a clique it's gonna be White Fence." I say, "That's pretty good, but I hope you didn't do nobody wrong." "No, I want to get in White Fence. I want to be one of the boys." "That's good enough for me. If you guys want to be in White Fence, it has to be on a Friday, 10 o'clock at night." And sure enough, they were there, man. This time there was six of them. They call them the Tiny Locos. *Chavalones* [kids]. Now they got their own clique in Baldwin Park.

Another man, from the Monstros, roughly the same age, glories in the strength of gang in their street hangout, just like a teenager: "On Saturday nights the neighborhood is full of them. Down there off Euclid, on the bottom of the Hill, from the bottom all the way to the dead end. Puro homies. It's big enough for a whole dance club. Rucas, vatos. The *jura* [cops] don't go down there, homes. They're scared."

In truth, these older men who hang around with the teenagers are what one of our staff of community researchers called "dinosaurs, roaming the streets long after their time is gone." Many of these men have little to their lives except the gang, and when they become involved with the adolescents their presence, and their stories, can't help but modify the cliques. How they do so, we don't know.

Toward a Typology of Ex–Gang Members: Tecatos, Cholos, and Squares

Obviously, there is a lot of variation among these men and women, and this parallels findings from other studies. In an early study of a black ghetto in Washington, D.C., for example, Hannerz (1969) identified four types of life-styles: first, mainstreamers; second, swingers (young single men and women); third, street families, headed by women; and finally, streetcorner men (peer-oriented men).

Our sample can also be divided into categories that reflect the realities of East Los Angeles life, which differ, of course, from those of black life in Washington. This typology is based partly on the ways in which respondents themselves categorize each other, and partly on respondents' lifelong patterns of work, family, peer, and drug-related behaviors.

First, paralleling Hannerz's "streetcorner men" are the classic tecatos described above. The men spend a good deal of their time in prison, and have neither job nor family lives. The women spend less time in prison, but have equally unstable family lives, sometimes keeping their children and sometimes relinquishing them to relatives.

Second, there is a category of men and women who seem never to have grown out of the gang. "Going down to the barrio" remains their way of life. For want of a better term, they might be called cholos. They have unstable work and family lives, usually continue some involvement with drugs (but seldom with the recurrent tecato prison time), or else are involved in other criminal activity that keeps them tightly tied to homeboys.

Both the tecatos and the cholos are people who have, in effect, failed to "mature out" of gang relationships and behaviors. Criminologists in the past have tended rather uncritically to assume that people grow out of youthful deviance: Crime and drug addiction, as well as gang involvements, are seen as young adult activities. However, in recent years, critical examination of the maturing out process suggests that outgrowing psychologically significant youthful deviance is conditional on a number of factors (see Anglin et al., 1986).

One type of gang member *does* mature out. Paralleling Hannerz's "mainstreamers" are what we call "squares." For men, the important criteria are steady job history, little involvement with serious drugs or prison, and a more or less steady family life. For women, jobs and prison are less important and family is more important.

Tecatos

Tecatos have been discussed extensively earlier in this chapter. To give more detail, they account for slightly more than a quarter of the male sample, and for a much smaller proportion of the female sample. About equal proportions are from earlier and from more recent cliques. The tecato lifestyle is an artifact of the long-standing heroin subculture in these neighborhoods, and whether it will persist depends largely on whether heroin continues to be an important drug.

Cholos

This category accounted for about a third of the men and somewhat more of the women. They were still holding on to the cholo values and behaviors of the adolescent gang, but they were not following the tecato path. Many were polydrug users, or used PCP or other serious drugs rather heavily, but tended to avoid the complete life-style involvement of the typical tecato. Some had served substantial prison terms, usually for nonnarcotics offenses. They continued to hang around with the boys (and/or girls). This is a mixed category: There are lots of different reasons for not growing up.

Many of these men and women were in considerable trouble as teenagers, and a few seemed to give rather disoriented responses—perhaps indicating psychological problems, or intoxication at the time of the interview. Paradoxically, for many of these people, the gang itself did not seem to be pivotal. A few seemed to seek out a gang as a place to act out their problems, joining rather late in adolescence. Such people had relatively little of the intense loyalty that characterized the more typical gang members. Some spent a good deal of their adolescence incarcerated, and had the distorted view of the gang that characterizes "state-raised" youth (see Moore et al., 1978). A few were frozen in gang values because of traumatic incidents—including one young man who was shot and paralyzed in the course of a robbery when he was 21. A few were from underclass families, some with addicted or imprisoned parents, and for them the gang and cholo life was a matter of course.

Few of these men and women had much job history. They relied on General Relief, hustling, relatives, and occasional jobs. Their life-style led to frequent firings from work—or to walking out of jobs that they did not like. Many went for years with no work at all. The men often lived with and depended on parents. Sometimes they lived with women or with other relatives (uncles, nephews) or homeboys just as feckless and drug-involved as themselves. (Those who depended on General Relief faced a number of restrictions on their living arrangements: Shared living quarters meant a reduction in the check.) One man summarized his recent living arrangements: "I was like jumping around. From my sister's to my mom's, cause my uncle didn't want me there because they shot up the house and stuff like that. Just like moving around here and there." The women also tended to work off and on, lived with relatives, got welfare, and occasionally lived with cholo men.

Marriages were also unstable, usually with an early marriage to a fellow gang member, followed by an early divorce. Marriage rarely interrupted the peer-oriented life-style of the men. But for women, teenaged motherhood tended to anchor them in the home, and the divorce permitted them to pick up where they left off partying. This often led to a kind of delayed adolescence. A 29-year-old woman, for example, had been married at 16 to a gang member. She had a child, but was divorced at 19; she left her child with her parents. She got a job, but was fired for unreliability; she dealt some drugs, and was still leading a chola life at the time of the interview. She describes her revitalized adolescence: "When I was 21 I was like a 16-year-old. I went backwards. When I was 16 I was more mature. At 19, when I got divorced, for the first time in my life I was going out." One 24-year-old White Fence woman with one child and a husband in prison, worked part-time as a bookkeeper. She described her involvement in street hangouts:

> I still hang around there. I still go there. With all the homeboys and homegirls. I still party with them to this day. I still smoke with them. They smoke Kools [cigarettes laced with PCP] all the time. We party—at the Lane, the Hole—all the time. I'm there half a day. After I go to my job, after, in the morning. I have to take care of business and then I'm there say from after 12 o'clock, I'm at the neighborhood.

Another 29-year-old White Fence chola on welfare, with several children, stated her priorities: "Me now that I'm an adult my kids are my
priority, but if it came down to it, I'll back [the gang] up. [Why do you
say that? How come you still feel like that?] Because it's part of our life.
Some just do it to get a kick out of it, but some of us have that even if
we try to change our lives or the way we dress. We still have that inside
of us."

Most of these men and women were from the recent cliques, and
we might expect these people either to mature out of their cholismo in
coming years or to become more confirmed in a street life-style. However, there are economic circumstances that militate against getting the
kind of stable jobs, available a generation ago, that would provide a reason
to mature out of the cholo life-style.

Squares

About 40 percent of the men and fewer women were leading conventional lives at the time of the interview, and had been doing so for some
time. A high proportion were from earlier cliques. Some rejected the
term "square" as describing them: One man commented, for example,
that the term might be appropriate for his parents, but that he himself
was a mixture—what he called "hip-square." Another, a younger man
who had earned a two-year associate's degree and had been working at
a state office for several years, also rejected the term: "I'm not square,
man. I know what's happening. You can take the homeboy out of the barrio, but you can't take the barrio out of the homeboy. That's where I'm
at." Our figures understate the proportions of square ex–gang members:
these were the people—especially women—who were most likely to
refuse to be interviewed (see the Appendix).

There is no single pathway to the square adaptation. Looking first at
the role in the gang, it is true that many men who are now square were
only peripherally involved in the gang. They were square even when they
were most active as teenagers—not going in for the more extreme gang
violence or drug use. For some, this was because concerned parents restricted them; others saw the gang simply as a neighborhood friendship
group, rather than as place to play out scenes of teenaged bravado. They
were square kids at heart, for whom gang membership was something of
an aberration.

Others, however, were actively into all of the gang locura—including several who defined themselves as the "black sheep" in otherwise respectable families. Some of these men just "walked away" from the gang after particularly traumatic events in adolescence. Others took on new roles in young adulthood that made the gang irrelevant—joining the Marines, or getting happily married to a conventional girl. It used to be something of a gang tradition for boys who feel their gang life getting out of control to join the military. For 11 percent of the men, like this Maravilla member, it was a major turning point in the teens: "I was getting in a lot of trouble; that's why I decided to get into the military. [Trouble?] Getting arrested or fighting, fights, you know what I mean. Gang activities, and, you know, taking reds, drinking. Then I decided to go into the Marines, to get away from the ghetto, from the barrio."

Others must be termed "reformed" tecatos—men who not only embraced gang locura during adolescence, but also became involved in drugs and/or prison. These people are rare. More common are men and women who continued the cholo life-style into their 20s or even into their 30s—losers who finally grew out of it. One 28-year-old White Fence woman had a short-lived marriage and four children, and had been mostly hanging around with her homegirls until she decided to take a test for a job with the police. She had been working at the job for seven months at the time of the interview, and saw it as a major turning point in her life:

> I was trying to find something. I felt like worthless until I found this job, you know, like I was never gonna accomplish nothing—just be on welfare, or something like that. . . . Just the thought of working for the police department, and being on the other side for once, it makes me feel a lot better about myself, you know. [That you feel pride in yourself?] Yeah, because I had to take a test and I feel at the top.

Many of these men and women, like this 29-year-old man, are quite reflective:

> [When did the change come about?] In my early 20s. [How did it come about?] I don't know. I think after you leave the neighborhood you start—you know you see different places, you see different things. There's other things out there. You start going to clubs, or you start going to different places, camping, vacations. You see

other things than the neighborhood. I mean there's nothing wrong with being in the neighborhood, but you find there's other things out there, too, to do with your time besides sitting around getting loaded.

Most of the men had worked quite consistently over the years. Some had remarkably steady jobs, working for fifteen, twenty, and sometimes thirty years for the same employer. These included a welder, a barber, a clerk in the district attorney's office, and a factory foreman. Some were clearly successful as well as stable. One man lost an arm in his 20s, decided to go to college, and became an accountant. Another got steady promotions in the same firm from 1955 till the firm closed in 1977, and then, after a brief spell as a truck driver, he became a proud owner-operator of a truck, and had been making good money for some five years.

Others were more precarious. One man married, had six children, and in his 40s built a reasonably successful construction company. "That's when things were good for me, in my 40s, because I got prosperous: I had a boat, I had a summer home in Ensenada, I became a grandfather. But in my 50s everything collapsed on me. I got divorced, lost my son, lost my business." He was diabetic, blind in one eye, and unemployed when interviewed. Another worked for eighteen years as a truck driver for a large firm, but when he was 38 he entered his third bad marriage and when it collapsed, so did he, and so did his job. When he was in his mid-forties he began several years of serious drinking—a fifth of brandy a day. When interviewed at the age of 49, he had remarried, was working again, going to school, and had been drinking very little. The personal problems experienced by these and other square men and women relate only minimally to the fact that they were formerly in gangs. Only when such problems send a man or woman back to the unreconstructed homeboys is a square adaptation jeopardized.

Women who became square after gang experience were usually those who stayed married, to a reasonably square man with a reasonably stable job, for a fairly long period of time. Marriage and children usually meant a break with the gang, and for these women—unlike the cholas—the break was permanent. Sometimes these women worked, and sometimes they did not. A few square women never married, but found stable jobs and continued to live with their parents.

Square women may be particularly underrepresented in our sample. Some such women refused the interview because their husbands would not allow them to discuss their "deviant" adolescence; others refused because they were afraid that they would be questioned about what they now defined as "deviance"—particularly about sexual activity. These views offer a poignant confirmation of the stigma attached to women's gang membership.

Summary

It is almost certain that the adult years of most gang members were rockier than those of their nongang peers in the neighborhoods. Most gang members had a history of marital instability, few men raised their own children, few attained job stability, and high proportions became involved in heroin use and the heroin street life-style. Three types of adaptation seem to prevail: tecatos, heroin addicts with an established street life-style; cholos, men and women who persist in gang involvement well into adulthood; and squares, who adopt a conventional life-style. Men and women of the earlier cliques were more likely to mature out of gang involvement and adopt a conventional life-style. This is only partly a function of the fact that they were older when they were interviewed. Some of the differences are a function of life-cycle differences, but in the next chapter I speculate about the extent to which changes in the neighborhoods and in the gangs have made it more difficult for these men and women to assume conventional adult roles.

chapter eight

Conclusion

This book has focused on change in two of Los Angeles' Chicano neighborhood gangs. We have discovered some very real changes over the years, but also some important continuities in the long history of the two gangs. What can be concluded from this study that is of generalizable interest?

Traditional Youth Gangs in a Period of Change

The gangs discussed in this book are like Chicano gangs found in many places in the Southwest, but they differ from most of the new gangs that have attracted both media and research attention since 1987. El Hoyo Maravilla and White Fence are old, long-standing, traditional gangs, with their own norms, traditions, and controls. They did not form for the purpose of making money out of drugs, like Detroit's black "corporate gangs" studied by Taylor (1990). They were not a product of recent economic catastrophe overlaid on an old racist political economy, like the black and Hispanic gangs of Milwaukee (Hagedorn, 1988). They did not, like some Puerto Rican gangs in Chicago, make a collective decision to move away from adolescent gang fighting into drug dealing (Padilla, 1990).

What have been the major changes since the 1950s? First, these gangs have in some ways become more entrenched—more institutionalized. Second, they are more influential and important in the lives of their members. Third, they have also become more deviant. In some respects, particularly sexuality, the broader adolescent culture has become more acting out since the 1950s: Gang members may still be within the range of "normal deviance" in sexuality. However, in two other aspects of their lives—drugs and violence—they have become more socially isolated. Since the early 1980s there has been a long-range decline in drug use among high school seniors, and this makes the continued high drug use among gang members more deviant. The high, though fluctuating, rate of lethal violence also means that the gangs are increasingly deviant. Finally, they have become more socially isolated from other adolescent peer groups in their communities, and are no longer tolerated by adults. Criminal-justice system labeling has contributed to this isolation. It is probably enhanced by the substantial influx of culturally conservative Mexicans into these communities; in the two neighborhoods we study, Mexican-born children generally stay away from the gangs. In sum, the gangs are no longer just at the rowdy end of the continuum of local adolescent groups—they are now really outside the continuum.

However, the real surprise for anyone whose expectations are molded by the media is that there has been so little change in the direction of deviance. These gangs are *not* the "crack gangs" that generated so much media attention. Many of the changes are subtle, difficult to extract. There is little that jumps out. This is particularly clear with regard to deviance. The adolescent cliques of the 1970s were involved in more deviant behavior than the cliques of the 1950s, and their alumni were more involved in illicit activity as adults than were the alumni of the gangs of the 1950s, but the differences are not dramatic.

Part of the explanation for the comparatively slow rate of change is that this is an old street culture. There has been substantial continuity between one clique and another since the 1940s. Researchers in other communities and other gangs report that the relationships between "old heads" and "young boys" have disintegrated (Anderson, 1990). But that is not true in East Los Angeles. Older men are generally respected by the younger ones: veteranos are still considered to be worth listening to, and "the neighborhood" remains a viable—often a coercive—concept. Extreme shifts in behavior don't seem to happen; stylistic fads—in clothing, drugs, or music—are slow to be adopted; adult drug dealers don't flaunt their money or their status in the neighborhood. Cocaine, when it became established in the late 1980s, did not suddenly oust heroin: Instead, it was used side by side with heroin. Thus the fate of older members becomes of major importance in understanding what has been happening to the gang in adolescence.

Gangs and Economic Restructuring

The data showed that there had been many changes in the neighborhoods and in the gangs that had nothing to do with the debate about the nature of poverty and a lot to do with the nature of gangs as "street" agencies of socialization during adolescence. But matters were different when it came to the question of "maturing out" of the gang.

Economic restructuring has taken "good" jobs away from East Los Angeles, and replaced them with exploitative jobs—unstable, low-wage, and unsheltered. Kin-based job networks that found decent work for earlier clique members deteriorated. Young adult gang men find themselves competing with immigrants. When asked why he didn't like a particular job, a 31-year-old man complained: "Well, I didn't like the way they were running it. After a while they started firing *la raza*—well, you know, the Chicanos—and hiring the border people. [They started hiring wetbacks?] Yeah, they started hiring them. Throwing us out. They give them a lower income. Not that I don't blame them for coming over and wanting some money, but. . . ."

One consequence, of course, is that young adult gang members have to find nonjob means of survival—and our data indicate that this means more dependence on transfer payments and illicit income. Increased job instability leads to changes in behavior. It prolongs the involvement with the homeboys and homegirls, and generates even greater instability in relationships with spouses.

Obviously, economic restructuring does not affect all types of gang members equally: The gang is not just a group of undereducated minority men and women. Some members, like the tecatos, the heroin addicts with an established street life-style, are *never* much affected by local economic opportunities. And squares who are prone to adopt a conventional life-style may still find conventional means to conventional careers. It is the cholos, the men and women who are likely to drift, who are most likely to be affected by changes in the opportunities to assume meaningful adult roles.

The fate of adults in the newly structured economy of the community is significant not only in and of itself. Because of the influence of the veteranos, the gang itself changes. The strongly demarcated social structure—the clique structure—begins to melt. More young adults find themselves going down to the barrio, hanging around—both with their age peers and with men and women from other cliques. Some show up regularly in the same street hangouts that attract adolescents. This retards their emotional maturation out of the gang. It also has an effect on the youngsters in the gang because it enhances the importance of the street socialization that takes place there. It also makes the gang seem even more like an accepting family, now with "older brothers" readily available. Gang veteranos are no longer remote figures—they are right there, and some even get involved in the affairs of younger cliques. Street socialization—quasi-institutionalized in the gang—becomes more competitive with conventional socialization, especially in the family and school.

How Important Are External Changes?

What we are suggesting is that at least in its youth phase this kind of traditional gang may be in some respects shielded from the direct effects of external changes. Of course, we cannot say what might have happened if certain external influences had been different. Thus gang programs in both neighborhoods seem to have had a conventionalizing effect in the past, but the programs have largely disappeared in recent years. There is little question that the gangs have become more deviant, but is it because gang programs have ceased to operate? What has been the effect of the unremitting pressure from police? How would the gangs have developed without those pressures?

The indirect effects of some external changes seem much clearer: Economic restructuring has probably expanded the street presence of veteranos, and this in turn has probably had a significant influence on the gangs. Up to this writing, the paucity of good jobs does not seem to have generated the kind of heavy illicit drug dealing that some gangs elsewhere have embraced. But will this continue? And because we can see no direct effects, we can only begin to speculate about the long-range impact of recent large-scale immigration from Mexico. These two gangs have remained almost entirely Chicano—but that means that they are increasingly unrepresentative of their neighborhoods.

The Future

What is likely to happen to these gangs in the future? Many of the circumstances that got these gangs started in the first place still persist (Vigil, 1982). The population of East Los Angeles is still marginalized in a variety of ways. The gangs have shown remarkable resilience in the face of heavy police pressure and of stylistic changes in the adolescent subculture that make the traditional cholo style look old-fashioned, and despite a discouraging dose of lethal violence. There were times in the last decade when some of our respondents doubted that the gangs would endure. Yet in spite of life-style changes and other pressures it seems likely that the gangs will continue to be significant agents of socialization for a small fraction of youth in these neighborhoods. We have suggested that those youth who join gangs tend to come from troubled families, and this is a population that is not likely to shrink. The children of Mexican immigrants may well find the cholo path attractive—or so some researchers (Vigil) believe. Further, it seems likely that gangs will also continue to be important to young adults from these and other poor communities. The United States is going through an unprecedented wave of incarceration, with a projected 68 percent increase between 1990 and 1995 (Austin and McVey, 1989). We have dealt extensively elsewhere (Moore et al., 1978) with the functions of gangs both in prison and for ex-inmates on the streets, and we have seen nothing in recent changes to cause us to modify our earlier analysis.[1]

It is easy for researchers interested in poverty to dismiss the gangs. Gangs have been *so* sensationalized, and some researchers have done little more than concentrate on the sensational aspects (e.g., Katz, 1988). But in an increasing number of inner-city neighborhoods, they are significant institutions of adolescent socialization. And they may have become increasingly important in the transition to young adulthood under changing economic conditions.

In some communities, they have become economic institutions as well—"ethnic enterprises," as Padilla (1990) puts it. They thus carry their "deviant" socialization into adulthood. However, though men and women from El Hoyo Maravilla and White Fence do find crime partners among their homeboys and homegirls, these two gangs have clearly *not* become economic institutions.

Many of their norms militate against such a transformation. And it may be that the social processes within the gang also militate against such a transformation. Anderson (1990) emphasizes the importance of "old heads" in street socialization of young adults ("young boys"), and he views with alarm the disappearing influence of such "old heads." We have documented the increased appearance of adults in the street hangouts of these two gangs. Certainly these veteranos do a disservice to the young gang members by perpetuating false values. But it may well be that such men and women, with all of their ludicrous attachment to adolescent values, are performing a useful function in helping maintain some of the traditional gang norms and thus fending off the possibilities of gangs' moving into corporate illicit activities. But it is the larger economic changes that have the greater impact on these gang members as they move into adulthood.

Girls in the Gang

Throughout this book, we have dealt evenly with gang women as well as men. Such even-handed treatment is clearly justified by the numbers: A full third of the people involved in the cliques we studied were females, and we suspect that gang women have more influence on their children than do gang men. But such even-handed treatment is virtually unknown in the literature on gangs. There are a few studies of gang girls that omit any discussion of boys, and a number of studies of "gangs" that actually turn out to be studies of boys in gangs.

Does the absence of research on girls in the gang mirror objective reality? Are the gangs we studied unique in having girls' cliques attached to them? Or is it a case of neglect? We cannot answer these questions directly with what we now know about gangs throughout the nation, but we do know that a number of studies of Chicano gangs in Los Angeles have concentrated on one gender to the exclusion of the other. This suggests that the neglect of the gender composition of the gang is systematic and structured.

Gang as Gender and Racial Stereotype:
Back to the Moral Panic

The media image of the gang is a stereotype. This is confirmed by the way in which gender is treated. The stereotyped gang is quintessentially male, with no place for women. Fighting is its quintessential activity. This stereotype is held as much by many of the gang boys as it is held by outsiders, as we have seen in Chapter Four. The closest gang boys come to acknowledging the presence of girls is the concept of the gang as "family," in which members take care of one another. That concept of "family," incidentally, is almost totally lacking from the media stereotype of gangs.

Stereotypes contribute to the "cognitive purification" of social cleavages (Connell, 1987). One such cleavage is gender: The gender realities of the gang are complicated, but the stereotype is clear and pure—and intensely male. This is what is meant by "cognitive purification": Gangs sharpen and simplify middle-class newspaper readers' notions of what lower-class maleness is. Every so often the media discover that there are girls in gangs and that girls can also be violent, but "gang as social concern" is pretty much all male. Perhaps for the image of "gang" to include girls as well as boys would be to humanize the gang too much, to force the audience to think of domestic relationships as well as pure male brute force. It might also challenge simplified and comfortable notions about women.

The stereotype of gangs also contributes to the cognitive purification of racial cleavages. Race is part of the image of gangs—and the stereotype is of violence and general criminality. Every so often the media discover gangs that are *not* black or Hispanic, and there's a brief flurry of interest before the return to the "real" problem—minority gangs. Perhaps for the image of "gang" to include whites as well as blacks and Hispanics would be to make Anglos think too much about gangs as ordinary adolescents, like their own children, not like "them."

To be sure there is a reality behind these stereotypes, but the realities are amplified. Stereotypes *always* represent amplification of reality. But the moral panics about gangs in the late 1980s obscured some of the basic economic changes that generated the national upsurge in gang and drug-marketing activity. To be sure, economic restructuring had vastly different effects on poorly educated minority populations in the devastated rustbelt cities than in the boomtown Southwest. Yet the increased unemployability of young men—so obvious in our sample— was a common denominator. Institutions develop where there are gaps in the existing institutional structure. Gangs as youth groups develop among the socially marginal adolescents for whom school and family do not work. Agencies of street socialization take on increased importance under changing economic circumstances, and have an increased impact on younger kids, whether they serve as beeper-driven flunkies for drug-dealing organizations or are simply recruited into an increasingly adult-influenced gang. Just how the specifics of economic restructuring play out from city to city and how the specifics affect different subcultural groups is a matter for future research.

Cliques in the Gang:
Sampling and Interviewing

Sampling

Our sample design reflected our interest in finding out about changes in these gangs over the years. In this appendix, we discuss the gang structure insofar as it bears on our sampling experiences. The gangs are age-graded, with separate cliques. Each clique is named, but each is part of the larger gang. In the Hoyo Maravilla gang there were eighteen male and eight female cliques between the "originals" and the cliques of the mid-1970s, and in the White Fence gang there were fourteen male and seven female cliques in that period. The names and beginning and ending dates for all of the cliques are given in Table 3-1.

Generally, only about half of the male cliques had female cliques affiliated with them. These girls' cliques also had names. (In other cases the girls that hung around the boys' cliques were less formally attached to the boys.) The girls in El Hoyo Maravilla had considerable autonomy. Thus although the Vamps started at about the same time as the male Cherries clique, the girls in the Vamps dated boys from the Jive Hounds as well as the Cherries. The girls in Las Cutdowns dated boys from the Dukes, the Tinies, and the Santos as well as the boys from the Lil Cutdowns clique; and the girls from Las Locas dated Peewees as well as Locos. At the outset of our study, we did not understand this quasi-autonomy, and chose Las Monas as the female counterpart to the male Midgets clique. It was not until well into the interviewing that we recognized that Las Monas was quite independent, and the Midgets had no female "auxiliary" at all. In fact, Las Monas was formed later than the Midgets, and was actually contemporary with the Lil Midgets, rather than the [Big] Midgets. This mistake reflects the substantial male-oriented bias in our original information: The information on which we drew was derived almost entirely from males, and though they knew every detail of male clique formation, what happened with the girls' cliques was not very interesting to them.

In previous studies we had collected information on each of these cliques from former members. We knew roughly when each clique originated and when it disintegrated, and how many individuals had been involved during the peak years of adolescent activity. We also had a roster of these members, as well as information on which of them had become addicted to heroin and which had been imprisoned. For male cliques, this information was derived from only two or three clique members, and from even fewer respondents from the women's cliques. Accordingly we considered this information to be only a starting point for drawing our samples.

There were several considerations in designing our sample. First, we wanted to interview women as well as men, and this meant that we were confined to those male cliques that had allied female cliques. It would have been virtually impossible to compile rosters of the loosely affiliated crowd of girls that simply hung around.

The second concern was that we interview in both earlier and more recent cliques, and we chose 1958 arbitrarily as a useful halfway mark. Cliques that formed prior to 1958 were classified as early cliques.

Finally, we were interested theoretically in how variations from one clique to another might affect behavior—and especially drug use. Accordingly, we drew on our rough information about heroin users and stratified the cliques in terms of whether the majority wound up using heroin. In Table A-1 the column labeled "Heroin Use" records the actual proportion of respondents in each clique who reported using heroin. The figures for male cliques generally corroborated our choices: Thus we had initially chosen the White Fence "Originals" as a clique in which our key informants said a minority used heroin and the White Fence Monsters as a clique in which the majority used heroin, and this initial choice was confirmed by our data.

In short, we first drew a sample of cliques. All of the male-female cliques in these two gangs were stratified on two theoretically relevant dimensions: epoch of formation and prevalence of heroin use. We chose eight cliques in all: four from each gang, each with an accompanying

Table A-1. Sampling Summary: Cliques and Characteristics

	N				
Name (date of origin)	Original Roster	Final Roster	Heroin Use[a]	Sample Target	Interviews Obtained
White Fence (WF)					
a. Early Cliques					
"Originals" (1944)	50	52	30.7%	17	13
Honeydrippers (Female)	23	24	12.5	8	7
Monsters (1946)	25	26	75.0	8	8
Lil White Fence (Female)	7	7	0	2	2
b. Recent Cliques					
Monstros (1968)	84	157	53.6	28	28
Monstras (Female)	25	67	11.1	9	9
Lil Termites (1972)	18	21	87.5	6	8
Lil Termites (Female)	6	7	100.0	2	2
Hoyo Maravilla (HM)					
a. Early Cliques					
Cutdowns (1946)	38	40	50.0	13	13
Jr. Vamps (Female)	9	10	33.3	3	3
Midgets (1950)	35	39	76.9	12	12
Monas (Female)	24	35	0	7	7
b. Recent Cliques					
Locos (1964)	24	38	66.7	8	9
Locas (Female)	31	31	20.0	10	10
Chicos (1967)	44	51	46.7	15	15
Chicas (Female)	6	6	⎧ 50.0	2	2
Ganzas (Female)	30	32	⎩	10	10
Totals: Male	318	424		107	106
Female	161	219		53	52
Both	479	643		160	158

[a] "Heroin use" records the proportion in each clique actually reporting heroin use. The following cliques were initially sampled as ones in which a majority used heroin: WF Monsters, WF Lil Termites, HM Midgets, and HM Locos.

female clique. Thus in each gang we had two earlier cliques, one in which the majority used heroin, and one in which only a minority used heroin. And in each gang we had two recent cliques, one in which the majority used heroin and one in which the minority used heroin. The cliques we drew are marked with asterisks in Table 3-1. After selecting the cliques, we made one additional departure from our clique plan. We found that there had been only six girls in the Hoyo Maravilla Chicas clique. One of our staff, who had been a Ganza, persuaded us that since the Chicas and Ganzas hung around together, and since they both dated male Chicos and Ganzos, we should pool the two girls' cliques. We did so.

Our next task was to draw samples of respondents from each of these cliques. We set a target at one-third of the original membership. Names were drawn randomly from our rosters of those original members. In Table A-1 we present those original sampling targets, along with the number of individuals listed in the rosters we had at the outset of the project. The final sample target was set at 107 males from an original total of 318 men listed in the rosters of members. And our women's sample target included 53 women out of an original total of 161 women listed in our original rosters. In the end, we interviewed a grand total of 106 men and 52 women.

Drawing a random sample of an informal and long-dissolved group is surely an unusual undertaking. There are several issues worth discussing about our sampling procedures and about who we actually interviewed. I will first discuss the adequacy of our original rosters and second, I will discuss sample attrition.

How accurate were our original rosters? Were these actually the members of the clique at its peak? Were there any others? How did we know? We verified these rosters by asking every new respondent to look over our roster of his/her clique and add or delete names. At the outset this was a demanding part of the project, especially for the women's cliques, because we had collected so little information about them. (It was also irritating because we had to redraw the sample as names were added.) As it turned out, in twelve of the sixteen cliques we interviewed, our original rosters were accurate to within one to four names added during the course of the interviewing. (Most of these additional names were of men or women who had been marginal to the gang.) Thus in most of the cliques, our original rosters and the target samples based on them were adequate.

In four cliques, however, we discovered significantly more names than those listed on our rosters. We did not adjust the sample *size* to accommodate additional names: we just added the new names to the draw. Thus our sample falls short accordingly (Table A-1).

Two of these were in El Hoyo Maravilla. One was a woman's clique—Las Monas—originally listed as having twenty-four members and actually having thirty-five. Our seven interviews from this clique were therefore an undersample. This underenumeration did not surprise us. In fact, we were surprised that most of the original rosters of women's cliques were as accurate as they proved to be. The second was one of the recent male cliques—the Chicos—originally listed as having forty-four members but actually having fifty-one members. Our sample of fifteen from this clique was an undersample. The additional Chicos were men who had dropped out of the gang at relatively young ages, and had been marginal. Their names had been omitted by earlier informants.

The other two underenumerated cliques were in White Fence. These were the Monstros and the related female clique, the Monstras. Here the underenumeration reflected a change in the structure of the clique rather than marginal members omitted by informants. The change took us some time to comprehend. This clique departed from the normal pattern of age-graded recruiting. Normally, male cliques recruit new members during a few years during adolescence (see Chapter Three), and all members are within a few years of each other in age. Occasionally a new member may be recruited in prison and diverge from the age pattern, but these have been infrequent.

Unlike all of the other cliques studied, however, the Monstros, formed in 1968, were still actively recruiting in 1985 from among teenagers in the neighborhood, as were the Monstras—their female counterpart. Reputedly the members who were doing most of the recruiting were unemployed young men who were actively involved in drug use and petty dealing, and they were attracting younger men through drug networks. Drugs included PCP and heroin.

Since we started by interviewing older Monstros who had ceased to be active with gang friends, we did not become aware of this pattern of continued recruitment until interviewing was well under way. The anomalies in this clique led us to investigate what was happening in other recent cliques of White Fence, and though this kind of continuous recruiting was *not* occurring in the Lil Termites (the other more recent clique that we sampled), it may have been occurring in at least one of the other comparatively recent White Fence cliques.

Over the previous decade, the White Fence gang had greatly expanded its territory. This may have facilitated the process of continuing recruiting, since the Monstros clique may have been fracturing. In addition, field work undertaken in 1988 by Robert Garcia (with John Long and Diego Vigil) indicates that the pattern may have been related to young men's incapacity to get work and mature out of youthful gang affiliations. Thus, this changed structure may have been part of the evolution of an underclass in this neighborhood.

There is another important question. How many of the names drawn in the first sample were actually interviewed? How many had to be replaced by other names, and why? These are questions of sample attrition and substitution. Sample attrition was substantial. A total of 367 contacts were made in order to obtain 158 interviews—a ratio of 2.3 contacts for every interview. Forty-three percent of the contacts resulted in interviews.

There was quite a bit of variation from one clique to another in sample attrition. The anomalous Monstros clique, for example, had a high rate of sample attrition and replacement, as did the small earlier girls' clique— Lil White Fence. Sources of attrition are shown in Table A-2. The most common was a failure to find respondents: Almost half of the "can't find" cases were again in the White Fence Monstros. As we said above, the clique had grown both in membership and in territory, and networks were so loose that respondents were difficult to find.

The second most common source of sample attrition was death. (Subtracting the deaths raises the rate of "successful" contacts from 43 to 51 percent.) Death was most significant in the earlier male cliques. A full quarter of all of the names sampled in the four earlier male cliques were of men who were reported to be dead. This is quite a high death rate for men who were generally only in their fifties in 1985. We can only speculate about the causes of death, but many, of course, lived very hard lives and were addicted to heroin, with often inadequate nutrition and a number of serious illnesses.

At one point we were urged to verify reported deaths by looking up death certificates. We could not do this, and the reasons are worth reporting. First, in many cases we did not have enough identifying information. Sometimes we had just the nickname by which he or she was known in

Table A-2. Sources of Sample Attrition

	Total Contacts	Inter- viewed	Ratio	Dead	Refused	Can't find	Other[a]
White Fence							
a. Early Cliques							
"Originals"	41	13	31.7	14	8	3	3
Honeydrippers	12	7	58.3	1	3	1	0
Monsters	19	8	42.1	3	1	1	6
Lil White Fence	7	2	25.0	0	0	6	0
b. Recent Cliques							
Monstros	100	28	28.0	8	10	33	21
Monstras	22	9	40.9	2	3	5	3
Lil Termites (m)	10	8	80.0	0	0	0	2
Lil Termites (f)	3	2	67.0	0	0	0	1
Hoyo Maravilla							
a. Early Cliques							
Cutdowns	31	13	41.9	7	3	5	3
Jr. Vamps	3	3	100.0	0	0	0	0
Midgets	33	12	36.4	8	3	6	4
Monas	10	7	70.0	3	0	0	0
b. Recent Cliques							
Locos	16	9	56.2	1	1	0	5
Locas	14	10	71.4	1	2	0	1
Chicos	26	15	57.7	3	3	1	4
Chicas	2	2	100.0	0	0	0	0
Ganzas	17	10	58.8	0	2	3	2
Totals	366	158	43.2	51	39	64	55

[a]"Other" includes twenty people who were incarcerated; thirteen who lived too far away to interview, were in the military, were too sick or disabled to respond; and two women whose husbands refused to let them be interviewed. It also includes eight notorious police informers. The organization routinely eliminated such individuals: Interviewer credibility with other respondents required this policy.

the clique. For example, several people mentioned that "Driver" of the Monstros died in "about 1982," but none of the people who mentioned his death knew his full name. More often the problem revolved around extremely common first and last names. Thus "John Garcia" is too common a name in Los Angeles county for us to distinguish a particular John Garcia without either birth date or middle name, and neither of those pieces of information was available to us. Second, in most cases the reports gave us only vague indications of the actual year the person died, for example, "it was in the '50s, maybe 1955 or 1956, I don't remember for sure." Thus in the end verification of deaths was done through relatives or individuals who had attended funerals.

What external evidence is there that despite attrition we have a reasonably good sample of these gang members? Our major concern was that we oversampled the kinds of people who were easiest to find. These include the "losers" who were still involved with gang and barrio networks. We undersampled three types of people who are likely to be among the more "successful" members.

First, there were the people who couldn't be found. (Extraordinary efforts were made by staff—collectively—to locate respondents. It was one of the most illuminating parts of the project.) With the exception of the anomalous thirty-eight Monstros and Monstras who couldn't be located, there were only 26 individuals, or 7 percent of all contacts. Second were people who moved out of town. They also are likely to have shed gang ties, and they amounted to thirteen individuals, or 3.6 percent of our contacts. Finally, many of our thirty-nine refusals came from men and women who were reasonably successful and did not want to recall their gang past; 11 percent of our contacts.

Summing it all up, 21.6 percent of our "failed" contacts were with people who *might* have been more successful than those we actually interviewed. On the other hand, the 51 deaths (14 percent of the "failed" contacts) may have occurred to those who were more immersed in street life. So our overall assessment is that our sample somewhat underreports the achievements of these former gang men and women.

Data Gathering

Generally, the research group that gathered these data worked collaboratively. That is, academics with substantial research experience in the study of Chicano gangs and addicts worked with interviewers who were former members of the target gangs and staff who were residents of the local community (see Moore, 1977; Moore et al., 1978). The process differs from the traditional ethnographic use of "key informants" or "indigenous ethnographers," although it shares much with these approaches (see Waldorf, 1980). Under the name "participatory research," a similar approach has come to be used in research with groups who are unfamiliar with or alienated from more traditional approaches. In our project, community staff participated with academic researchers in all phases of the research, from design of instruments through the write-up of the final report.

In this project, staff orientation began during the second month of the project. The history of the project group was discussed along with the purpose of the current study. Staff did quite a bit of role-playing in order to overcome worries about some unusually sensitive questions used in our interview guide, for example, questions about incest.

The questionnaire was pretested by having interviewers interview ex–gang member staff members. The academic staff sat in on these interviews. In later consultation with the ex–gang member staff they modified the interview to better attain the project's goals.

The completed interview guide contained twelve parts. It began with a "residential time line," in which we recorded details (by five-year intervals) on where the respondent lived, who else lived there, who took the leading role, who worked, and what the jobs were, and what other sources of income (licit and illicit) were coming into the household. The second section obtained information about the family of origin, including parental characteristics and behavior and pathologies (illness, death, addiction, alcoholism, and incarceration) in the family. The third section focused on the respondent's runaway experiences, and then the interview moved on to the characteristics of the clique and of the respondent's best friends in the clique. This also included extensive questions about activities and values in the clique and a set of questions about the respondent's own experiences in the gang. Then we turned to the respondent's drug history, including heroin, on a year-by-year basis. Summary questions about the use of drugs followed. We then turned to questions about the timing of major life events, including the "best age" and actual age of occurrence, along with probes about the consequences of "off-timeness." We included a series of attitudinal questions that we had used in a previous study of women heroin addicts: Most focused on gender role expectations. Then we turned to the respondent's family of procreation, repeating some questions about behavior pathologies. We included a section on employment and job-finding behavior, and concluded with a set of attitudinal questions relating to political efficacy and to perceptions of drugs and prison.

Interviewing began in December 1984 and was concluded in the spring of 1985. Interviews were lengthy, lasting from three to five hours. Respondents were paid $20 for their participation.

chapter one: Introduction

1. In several instances, reporters became disenchanted with police releases. Bob Baker of the *Los Angeles Times*, for example, bypassed police channels for a series of interviews with gang members (see *Los Angeles Times*, June 26, 1988). He soon recognized that black gangs were very different from Chicano gangs, and did a separate report on Chicano gangs on December 11, 1988 (Personal communication, September 1988).

2. The *Los Angeles Times Index* shows gang entries as follows: 1972—32 entries (19 on Chicano gangs); 1973—18 entries (9 Chicano); 1974—9 entries (8 Chicano); 1975—9 entries (6 Chicano); 1976—13 entries (5 Chicano); 1977—36 entries (23 Chicano); 1978—15 entries (11 Chicano); 1979—18 entries (10 Chicano); 1980—25 entries (0 Chicano); 1981—68 entries (0 Chicano); 1982—55 entries (ethnicity not determinable from *Index*); 1983—49 entries (ethnicity not determinable); 1984—60 entries (ethnicity not determinable); 1985—59 entries (ethnicity not determinable); 1986—44 entries (2 Chicano); 1987—69 entries (8 Chicano); 1988—267 (18 Chicano); 1989—184 (ethnicity not determinable).

Without photographs, readers needed to infer from names whether black, Chicano, or Asian gangs were involved. In every year, a small fraction of the news items referred to events in other cities. From 1972 to 1979, items on Chicano gangs frequently were positive (community activities, school educational programs, and the like).

3. Interestingly, very few analysts were repeating the optimistic theme of the 1960s, that is, that minority gangs would become a revolutionary vanguard (see Chapters Four and Five).

4. Police, however, were well aware of the difference. Thus Jackson

and McBride (1985), Los Angeles law-enforcement gang specialists, call the Chicano gangs "traditional," in contrast to the black gangs.

5. This approach has been utilized by other gang researchers as well (see Hagedorn, 1988; Vigil, 1989).

chapter two: The Setting

1. Citrus, motion pictures, petroleum, and tourism were the important industries.

2. Schools were a continuous source of discontent within the Mexican-American community, with an early victory won in 1945 and 1946 when segregation was struck down (Romo, 1983).

3. Although this pattern continued in Boyle Heights through the early 1960s, rates in unincorporated East Los Angeles were comparable to those elsewhere in the county (Freudenberg and Street, 1965). Rates of "pre-delinquency" were higher. This refers to cases of "improper companions, runaways, truancy," and other "delinquent tendencies." Rates for the county as a whole were 4.5 per 1,000; for Boyle Heights they were 10.2 per 1,000, and for East Los Angeles they were 6 per 1,000. Rates of "delinquency," which required court action, were also higher. For the county as a whole the rate was 11.2 per 1,000; in Boyle Heights they were 19.9 per 1,000, and in East Los Angeles 13.4 per 1,000. However, for "neglect petitions" (filed against parents and reflecting "inadequate parental care") rates were lower in these two neighborhoods. For the county as a whole the rates were 1.7 per 1,000; for Boyle Heights 1.6 per 1,000, and for East Los Angeles 1.0 per 1,000 (Freudenberg and Streets, 1965:6, C-1, C-3).

4. In 1955, three quarters of the aerospace employees were production workers but by 1961 only 54 percent were (Lane, 1975:21).

5. Land near East Los Angeles cost two to three times land located on the edges of the city, and new plants did not locate there.

6. In his study of minority representation in twenty-eight of Los Angeles' unions in 1950, Greer (1959) found that Mexicans were strongly represented (30 percent or more of the membership) in the following international unions: Cement Finishers, Packinghouse Workers (both AFL and CIO), Furniture Workers (both AFL and CIO), International Ladies Garment Workers, Building Laborers, and Dishwashers. Out of twenty-one local unions they were 30 percent or more of the membership in the following: Cement Finishers, Furniture Workers (Independent, AFL, and CIO), Utility Workers, International Ladies Garment Workers, Packinghouse Workers (AFL only), United Brick and Clay Workers, and Building Laborers.

7. By 1980, however, the income distribution in Los Angeles County was almost identical to that of the nation as a whole.

8. Perhaps the best known of the "land grabs" affecting Mexican Americans was outside of East Los Angeles, in the area north of downtown known then as the Palo Verde barrio. It is now known as Chavez Ravine—the home of the Los Angeles Dodgers Stadium. In 1951 the city housing authority condemned the land, most of which was occupied by Mexican Americans who were living in cheap housing much like that of East Los Angeles. Their first plan was to construct public housing, but when that plan fell through the land was offered to the Dodgers. Residents mounted a series of futile protests, and the last resident was forcibly removed and her home bulldozed early in 1959. The protests generated much more publicity than did the land-grab problems in East Los Angeles.

9. Until the time of Chief Parker, in 1950, the Los Angeles Police Department was notably subject to political interference, scandal-ridden, and only partly professionalized. In fact, Parker was the first chief of police since 1913 to survive a change in mayor. The department had a history of red-baiting. Industrial interests depended on them to keep labor agitators under control, and there were continual charges that they were used as strikebreakers. Notably, after the *Los Angeles Times* was bombed early in the century by IWW agitators, they constantly looked on the police as a bastion of free labor. A Red Squad was established in the department in the late 1930s for antilabor activities and to keep track of subversives.

The police force that stood by and even encouraged marauding servicemen during the Zoot-Suit Riots of 1943 was badly demoralized, underpaid, and under strength. When the riots began, there were fewer policemen than in 1925 (2,112 as compared with 2,500 in 1925) and at the same pay as in 1926. Many were, in fact, temporary replacements for wartime enlistments (Woods, 1973).

10. "Poverty" refers to the proportions living at or below 125 percent of the official poverty line; 1980 data about the communities in this section were obtained from special tabulations made by the Los Angeles United Way. I am grateful to the organization's research director, Marge Nichols, for her generous access to these data.

11. Eighteen percent of the school-aged children in these communities were monolingual Spanish speakers.

12. "Low-wage" manufacturing included apparel, textile, furniture, leather, and lumber; "moderate-wage" manufacturing included fabricated metals, chemicals, electrical machinery, primary metals, stone, clay, and glass; "high-wage" manufacturing included paper products, food processing,

transportation equipment, and printing (McCarthy and Valdez, 1986:40).

13. As Sassen notes (1988:161), 75 percent of the workers in the most unionized industries lost their jobs between 1978 and 1988. These industries included auto production, rubber tires, auto glass, steel, and steel products. By contrast, some 80,000 jobs were created in the garment industry.

14. The term "Hispanic" is used generally when the national origin is unknown. Thus in the period discussed here, these jobs in Los Angeles were often filled by undocumented workers from Central America as well as Mexico.

15. In 1980, 31 percent of Mexican-American teenaged boys and 25 percent of teenaged Chicanas were working in manufacturing jobs, as compared with 15 percent of teenaged Anglo boys and 9 percent of teenaged Anglo girls. Data from special tabulations of 1 percent PUMS (Public Use Micro Samples) sample, provided through the courtesy of Rebecca Morales, UCLA.

16. The "city" was developed as an administrative convenience to deliver low taxes for business. Very few people actually live there.

17. Soja et al. (1984:222) noted that "of the over 200 U.S. firms listed in a recent congressional hearing as having factories in the Mexican border towns of Tijuana, Tecate, and Ensenada, approximately 50% were headquartered in Los Angeles. They include not only such giant corporations as Hughes Aircraft, Northrop and Rockwell but dozens of small firms involved in apparel, food processing, auto parts, and electronics."

18. In 1980, in California Mexican-American husband-wife households, 16 percent with full-time working husbands fell below the poverty line, and 48 percent earned incomes that fell at less than twice the poverty level. Comparable figures for blacks were 5 and 27 percent, and for Anglos, 4 and 15 percent (James Geschwender, SUNY, Binghamton, special tabulations). And nationally, 1 out of every 15 Hispanics who worked year round and full-time fell below the poverty level in 1985, compared with 1 out of every 22 blacks and 1 out of every 40 whites (Center on Budget and Policy Priorities, 1986).

19. This discussion follows Acuña's narrative (1984), derived from content analysis of two Eastside newspapers.

chapter three: Two Barrio Gangs

1. Historical material on El Hoyo gangs was compiled in part by Jimmy Provencio and Steve Contreras.

2. Although the term cholo historically alluded to culturally marginal

mestizos (Vigil, 1988a) or to scoundrels and "half-breeds" (Pitt, 1966), it has come to refer primarily to the gang-oriented street style of dress and of walking and talking. See Vigil (1988a) for a full analysis of the cholo style.

3. The Special Services for Groups was incorporated as a private agency in 1952, following up on the Special Services unit that had been established in 1945. The organization continued through the 1960s, serving both White Fence and El Hoyo Maravilla in teen posts.

4. The YMCA was to reopen in White Fence in 1990, but was reportedly very resistant to working with the gang. A city playground also provided a place for White Fence members to work out and hang out, but as described in Chapter Two, the construction of a freeway barred the boys' access to this playground and after a series of gang fights it became acknowledged as part of the territory of the Varrio Nuevo gang. Later, the tunnel (under a freeway) that provided Varrio Nuevo youth with access to the playground was closed, and it once again became a White Fence hangout—under the careful supervision of a playground director who also happened to live across the street.

5. In the late 1980s there was much publicity about a "gradual continual decline in drug use in mainstream America" among the nation's teenagers (Lloyd Johnston, quoted in *New York Times*, July 10, 1988, E5). What was seen as "decline" is a 4.7 percent drop in the use of marijuana by high school seniors between 1975 and 1987, and a 4.8 percent drop in the use of hallucinogens. During the same period, the population surveyed increased the use of cocaine by 4.7 percent and of alcohol by almost 1 percent, from 84.8 percent in 1975 to 85.7 percent in 1987. Clearly many of even these most conformist of American adolescents—those who stayed in high school till their senior year—were still involved with alcohol and also with marijuana (36.3 percent). The peak year for marijuana was 1979, with 50.8 percent using.

6. More sophisticated law enforcement views Chicano gangs as "traditional," with membership a matter of family inheritance (see Jackson and McBride, 1985). In fact, direct family transmission of gang membership is a rarity, as discussed below.

chapter four: Changes in the Gangs

1. As I discuss in Chapter Seven, there is a good reason for this: first, most of the gang men do *not* want their children in a gang; second, most of the men who remain actively interested in the gang fail to rear their own children, and their influence is minimal.

2. A particular family of dealers is credited with being the first to introduce heroin dealing into El Hoyo, in 1947. Before that time, heroin users had to go downtown to get their drug.

3. The "phasing off" among women often involved the search for a protector, as this older Maravilla woman commented: "Some of them [started heroin] young, 14, 15. [?] When they were real hooked, they went off on their own. [?] Well they had to find someone that would help them with their habit."

4. In general, there was about a two-year standard deviation in these ages, except among the older women, who show a standard deviation of 5.2 years. The ages given by members of the younger cliques are notably earlier than figures given by a national sample of Hispanic respondents who came to maturity in the late 1970s and early 1980s. By the age of 15, 18.3 percent of the Hispanic males had sexual experiences, compared with 12.5 percent of white males and 44.3 percent of black males. And by the age of 17, only 28.5 percent of the Hispanic females had sexual experience compared with 31.3 percent of white females and 45.7 percent of black females (Mott and Haurin, 1988).

5. Statistics on gang homicide are peculiar. Chicago traditionally has counted a homicide as "gang-related" only if the investigating officers can clearly establish a gang motive for the killing. However, until 1989 Los Angeles police and sheriffs released statistics that counted as "gang-related" all homicides in which either the victim or the offender was identified by investigating officers as a gang member. This, of course, greatly exaggerated the number of homicides counted as gang-related. Release of statistics usually coincided with efforts by police to obtain new funding. When Los Angeles police decided to shift to the more restrictive definition (the "Chicago definition") they explained that they were doing so in order to reflect the successful efforts of law enforcement to combat gang violence.

6. Spearman's r = −.68.

7. Researchers generally agree that the gangs of the 1970s and 1980s were more violent than those of the 1950s and 1960s (Klein and Maxson, 1987; Miller, 1975). Miller (1975) argued that increased weaponry and the increased mobility that comes with car ownership were new factors, and Spergel (1986) added that the increased age of gang members is an additional factor.

8. Drive-by shootings later spread to other cities. They should not be confused with the infamous impersonal freeway shootings of the late 1980s, which did not involve gang members.

9. Spearman's r = .67.

10. Spearman's r = .68.
11. Spearman's r = .72.
12. Gang banging as used in this text refers to gang fighting.

chapter six: Gang Members' Families

1. But even the earlier studies concluded that family breakup per se might not be as damaging to a child as endemic family discord. Under certain circumstances breaking up a bad marriage might actually be an improvement for the child. Later studies confirmed this view (Kaplan and Pokorny, 1971).

2. Even researchers less wedded to a personality view of delinquency emphasize the importance of the family. Thus Mancini (1980), adopting a symbolic-interactionist approach, finds "strategic styles" of relating to others to be of great importance in distinguishing delinquent from nondelinquent slum teenagers. These styles, of course, are generated in the family, and reinforced by interactions in both peer group and school.

3. Overall, respondents remember that two-thirds of the Mexican-born parents took on American citizenship. This is a rate considerably higher than the usual rate of naturalization for Mexicans. According to McCarthy and Valdez, only 56 percent of California's Mexican immigrants entering before 1950 were naturalized by 1980 (1986:32). Mexican-born parents of younger clique members were significantly more likely than parents of older clique members to be naturalized: 83 percent of younger men's fathers, for example, compared with 62 percent of older men's fathers.

4. Seven variables were dichotomized and combined to form a global "Mexican ethnicity" score. These variables were: (1) father was born in Mexico; (2) mother was born in Mexico; (3) Spanish was the normal language at home; (4) use of English in the home was frowned upon; (5) father was considered head of the household with no questions; (6) father controlled mother's visitors; (7) respondent felt "Mexican" (as compared with "Chicano," "Mexican American," "confused," etc.). This global measure showed that younger cliques were significantly less "Mexican," and women were generally less "Mexican" at all ages.

5. Some indication of the long-range effects of the family may also be gleaned from answers to the question, "Which of your brothers and sisters was most successful?" Almost none said that nobody had been successful. A few hinted at a miserable family by singling out as "successful" a brother or sister who had avoided the street life (i.e., were drug-free), while a few were equivocal, citing the successful siblings' kindness and helpfulness. But

a good three-quarters—men and women, old and young—used good jobs, money, and material possessions as their indicators of success. And, as I discuss later, many of these respondents, gang members though they were, also turned out reasonably well.

chapter seven: Growing Up

1. This charge stems from arguments that needle track marks are indications that the individual has been using heroin. In recent years, the charge has fallen into disfavor, and heroin addicts are now arrested for being "under the influence."

2. Men from the older cohorts were married at a median age of 25.2; younger men at 20.2. Women—older and younger—were married at a median age of 18.

3. Older men were significantly more likely to work in firms with just a few employees (30 percent as compared with 15 percent of the younger men).

4. Most of the younger men (55 percent) and women (75 percent) had held their jobs for less than a year at the time of the interview.

5. Fifty-seven percent of younger men and 63 percent of older men worked during their early 20s and 81 percent of younger men but 65 percent of older men worked during their late 20s.

6. Interestingly, the men from recent cliques were *less* likely than men from the early cliques to have been imprisoned during their late 20s—33 percent compared with 46 percent. Slightly more than half of the men spent time in prison during their 30s, with no difference between men from older and from more recent cliques. Of course, few of the men from younger cliques had reached the age of 30.

7. About 55 percent of both older and younger women were working during their early 20s, and 60 percent of older and 67 percent of younger women were working during their late 20s. The latter difference is not statistically significant.

chapter eight: Conclusion

1. The major difference is that prisons of the 1980s and 1990s were considerably less likely to house strong inmate organizations. In our earlier analysis, we found these organizations playing an important and constructive role.

Acuña, Rodolfo. 1981. *Occupied America*. New York: Harper and Row.
———. 1984. *A Community under Seige*. Los Angeles: UCLA Chicano Studies Research Center Publications, monograph no. 11.
Aichhorn, August. 1935. *Wayward Youth*. New York: Meridian Books.
Anderson, Elijah. 1990. *Streetwise*. Chicago: University of Chicago Press.
Anglin, Douglas, M. L. Brecht, Arthur Woodward, and Douglas Bonett. 1986. "An Empirical Study of Maturing Out: Conditional Factors." *The International Journal of the Addictions* 21:233–46.
Austin, James, and Aaron McVey. 1989. *The 1989 NCCD Prison Population Forecast: The Impact of the War on Drugs*. San Francisco: National Council on Crime and Delinquency.
Baker, Bob. 1988. "Chicano Gangs: A History of Violence." *Los Angeles Times*, December 11, p. 1.
Balderrama, Francisco. 1982. *In Defense of La Raza:* Tucson: University of Arizona Press.
Beschner, George, and James Walters. 1985. "Just Another Habit? The Heroin User's Perspective on Treatment." In *Life with Heroin*, by Bill Hanson, George Beschner, James Walters, and Elliott Bovelle. Lexington, Mass.: Lexington Books.
Bogardus, Emory. 1926. *The City Boy and His Problems: A Survey of Boy Life in Los Angeles*. Los Angeles: Rotary Club.
———. 1943. "Gangs of Mexican-American Youth." *Sociology and Social Research* 28:55–66.
Brown, W. K. 1978. "Black Female Gangs in Philadelphia." *International Journal of Offender Therapy and Comparative Criminology* 21:221–28.
California, State of, Health and Welfare Agency, Employment Development

Department. 1989. *Annual Planning Information: Los Angeles–Long Beach Metropolitan Statistical Area (Los Angeles County)*. Los Angeles: Employment Development Department.

Campbell, Anne. 1984. *The Girls in the Gang*. Oxford: Basil Blackwell.

Carr, Jim, Jim Guerin, Bob Heffner, Karin Pally, Mary Beth Welch. 1985. "A Community Economic Development Study of Unincorporated East Los Angeles." Manuscript.

Casavantes, Edward J. 1976. *El Tecato: Cultural and Sociologic Factors Affecting Drug Use among Chicanos*. Washington, D.C.: National Coalition of Spanish Speaking Mental Health Organizations.

Center on Budget and Policy Priorities. 1986. "Hispanic Poverty Rises in 1985." Washington, D.C.: Center on Budget and Policy Priorities.

Cloward, Richard, and Lloyd Ohlin. 1960. *Delinquency and Opportunity*. New York: Free Press.

Cohen, Albert. 1955. *Delinquent Boys: The Culture of the Gang*. Glencoe, Ill.: Free Press.

Cohen, Stanley. 1980. *Folk Devils and Moral Panics: The Creation of the Mods and Rockers*. Oxford, Eng.: Martin Robertson.

Connell, R. W. 1987. *Gender and Power*. Stanford, Calif.: Stanford University Press.

Corrigan, Paul. 1979. *Schooling the Smash Street Kids*. London: Macmillan.

Crider, Raquel, Joseph Groerer, and Ann Blanken. 1989. "Black Tar Heroin Field Investigation." Rockville, Md.: National Institute on Drug Abuse.

Dieppa, Ismael. 1973. "The Zoot Suit Riots Revisited: The Role of Private Philanthropy in Youth Problems of Mexican Americans." Ph.D. diss., University of Southern California.

Dinitz, Simon, Frank Scarpitti, and Walter Reckless. 1962. "Delinquency Vulnerability: A Cross Group and Longitudinal Analysis." *American Sociological Review* 17:515–17.

Dwoskin, Sidney. 1948. "Developing Socialization of Adolescents by the Group Guidance Unit of the Delinquency Prevention Division of the Los Angeles County Probation Department." M.A. thesis, University of Southern California.

Eaton, Joseph, and Kenneth Polk. 1961. *Measuring Delinquency: A Study of Probation Department Referrals*. Pittsburgh, Pa.: University of Pittsburgh Press.

Erlanger, Howard. 1979. "Estrangement, Machismo, and Gang Violence." *Social Science Quarterly* 60:235–48.

Fine, Gary Alan. 1987. *With the Boys*. Chicago: University of Chicago Press.

Fishman, Laura. 1988. "The Vice Queens: An Ethnographic Study of Black Female Gang Behavior." Paper presented at the American Society of Criminology, University of Vermont, Burlington.

Fox, Rona. 1970. "The Brown Berets: A Participant Observation Study of Social Action in the Schools of Los Angeles." Ph.D. diss., University of Southern California.

Freudenberg, Edward, and Lloyd Street. 1965. *Social Profiles: Los Angeles County*. Los Angeles, Calif.: Welfare Planning Council, research report no. 21.

Frias, Gus. 1982. *Barrio Warriors: Homeboys of Peace*. Los Angeles: Diaz Publications.

Garbarino, James, Cynthia Schellenbach, and Janet Sebes. 1986. *Troubled Youth, Troubled Families*. New York: Aldine.

Garcia, Mario. 1985. "Americans All: The Mexican American Generation and the Politics of Wartime Los Angeles, 1941–1945." In *The Mexican American Experience*, edited by Rodolfo De La Garza, Frank Bean, Charles Bonjean, Ricardo Romo, and Rodolfo Alvarez. Austin: University of Texas Press.

Glueck, Sheldon, and Eleanor Glueck. 1934. *One Thousand Juvenile Delinquents*. Cambridge, Mass.: Harvard University Press.

Goldstein, Paul, et al. 1987. *Drug Related Involvement in Violent Episodes. Interim Final Report*. New York: Narcotic and Drug Research, Inc., and New York State Division of Substance Abuse Services.

González, Alfredo. 1981. "Mexican/Chicano Gangs in Los Angeles." Ph.D. diss., University of California—Berkeley.

Greer, Scott. 1959. *Last Man In: Racial Access to Union Power*. Glencoe, Ill.: Free Press.

Griffith, Beatrice. 1948. *American Me*. Boston: Houghton Mifflin.

Gustafson, Floyd V. 1940. "An Ecological Analysis of the Hollenbeck Area of Los Angeles." M.A. thesis, University of Southern California.

Hagedorn, John. 1988. *People and Folks: Gangs, Crime and the Underclass in a Rustbelt City*. Chicago: Lake View Press.

Hannerz, Ulf. 1969. *Soulside*. New York: Columbia University Press.

Harris, Mary. 1988. *Cholas: Latino Girls and Gangs*. New York: AMS Press.

Hawkins, J. D., D. M. Lishner, and R. F. Catalano. 1985. "Childhood Predictors and the Prevention of Adolescent Substance Abuse." In *Etiology of Drug Abuse: Implications for Prevention*, edited by C. L. Jones and R. J. Battjes. Rockville, Md.: National Institute on Drug Abuse, research monograph 56.

Healy, William, and Augusta Bronner. 1936. *New Light on Delinquency, and Its Treatment*. New Haven, Conn.: Yale University Press.

Horowitz, Ruth. 1983. *Honor and the American Dream*. New Brunswick, N.J.: Rutgers University Press.

Huff, C. Ronald. 1988. "Youth Gangs and Public Policy in Ohio: Findings and Recommendations." Paper presented at the Ohio Conference on Youth Gangs and the Urban Underclass, Ohio State University, Columbus.

Jackson, Robert K., and Wesley McBride. 1985. *Understanding Street Gangs*. Los Angeles, Calif.: Custom Publishing Co.

Jorquez, Jaime. 1984. "Heroin Use in the Barrio: Solving the Problem of Relapse, or Keeping the Tecato Gusano Asleep." *American Journal of Drug and Alcohol Abuse* 10:63–75.

Kaplan, Howard, and A. D. Pokorny. 1971. "Self Derogation and Childhood Broken Home." *Journal of Marriage and the Family* 33:328–37.

Katz, Jack. 1988. *Seductions of Crime*. New York: Basic Books.

Klein, Malcolm. 1971. *Street Gangs and Street Workers*. Englewood Cliffs, N.J.: Prentice Hall.

Klein, Malcolm, and Cheryl Maxson. 1987. "Street Gang Violence." In *Violent Crime, Violent Criminals*, edited by Marvin Wolfgang and Neil Weiner. Beverly Hills, Calif.: Sage.

Klein, Malcolm, Cheryl Maxson, and Lea Cunningham. 1988. *Gang Involvement in Cocaine "Rock" Trafficking*. Final Report for the National Institute of Justice. Los Angeles: University of Southern California, Social Science Research Institute.

Kornblum, William. 1987. "Ganging Together: Helping Gangs Go Straight." *Social Issues and Health Review* 4:98–118.

Lane, Thomas. 1975. "Report on Manufacturing Employment in the Los Angeles Region." M.A. thesis, University of California—Los Angeles.

Lees, Sue. 1986. *Losing Out*. London: Hutchinson.

Long, John. 1990. "Drug Use Patterns in Two Los Angeles Barrio Gangs." In *Drugs in Hispanic Communities*, edited by Ronald Glick and Joan Moore. New Brunswick, N.J.: Rutgers University Press.

Loya, Fred, Phillip Garcia, J. Sullivan, Luis Vargas, Nancy Allen, and James Mercy. 1986. "Conditional Risks of Homicide among Anglo, Hispanic, Black and Asian Victims in Los Angeles, 1970–1979." *Report of the Secretary's Task Force on Black and Minority Health*. Vol. 5, *Homicide, Suicide, and Unintentional Injuries*. Washington, D.C.: U.S. Department of Health and Human Services.

McCarthy, Kevin, and R. B. Valdez. 1986. *Current and Future Effects of Mexican Immigration in California*. Santa Monica, Calif.: Rand Corporation.

McWilliams, Carey. 1943. "Los Angeles' Pachuco Gangs." *New Republic* 108: 76–77.

————. 1949. *North from Mexico*. New York: Greenwood Press.

Mancini, Janet. 1980. *Strategic Styles: Coping in the Inner City*. Hanover, N.H.: University Press of New England.

Mazón, Mauricio. 1985. *The Zoot-Suit Riots: The Psychology of Symbolic Annihilation*. Austin: University of Texas Press.

Meeker, Marcia, with J. Harris. 1964. *Background for Planning*. Los Angeles, Calif.: Welfare Planning Council, research report no. 17.

Miller, Walter B. 1958. "Lower Class Culture as a Generating Milieu of Gang Delinquency." *Journal of Social Issues* 14:5–19.

————. 1975. *Violence by Youth Gangs and Youth Gangs as a Crime Problem in Major American Cities*. Washington, D.C.: U.S. Department of Justice, National Institute for Juvenile Justice and Delinquency Prevention, Office of Juvenile Justice and Delinquency Prevention.

Mirande, Alfredo. 1987. *Gringo Justice*. Notre Dame, Ind.: Notre Dame Press.

Moore, Joan W. 1977. "A Case Study of Collaboration: The Chicano Pinto Research Project." *Journal of Social Issues* 33:144–58.

————. 1985. "Isolation and Stigmatization in the Development of an Underclass: The Case of Chicano Gangs in East Los Angeles." *Social Problems* 33: 1–12.

————. 1988. "Variations in Violence among Hispanic Gangs." In *Proceedings: Research Conference on Violence and Homicide in Hispanic Communities*, edited by Jess Kraus, Susan Sorenson, and Paul Juarez. Los Angeles: University of California—Los Angeles.

————. 1990. "Mexican American Women Addicts: The Influence of Family Background." In *Drug Use in Hispanic Communities*, edited by Ronald Glick and Joan Moore. New Brunswick, N.J.: Rutgers University Press.

Moore, Joan, with Mary Devitt. 1989. "The Paradox of Deviance in Addicted Mexican American Mothers." *Gender and Society* 3:53–70.

Moore, Joan, with Robert Garcia, Carlos Garcia, Luis Cerda, and Frank Valencia. 1978. *Homeboys: Gangs, Drugs and Prison in the Barrios of Los Angeles*. Philadelphia: Temple University Press.

Moore, Joan, and Diego Vigil. 1987. "Chicano Gangs: Group Norms and

Individual Factors Related to Adult Criminality." *Aztlán* 18:27–44.

Moore, Joan, Diego Vigil, and Robert Garcia. 1983. "Residence and Territoriality in Chicano Gangs." *Social Problems* 31:182–94.

Morales, Armando. 1972. *Ando Sangrando (I Am Bleeding)*. La Puente, Calif.: Perspectiva Publications.

Morales, Rebecca. 1985. "Transitional Labor: Undocumented Workers in the Los Angeles Automobile Industry." *International Migration Review* 17:570–96.

Morales, Rebecca, and Paul Ong. 1988. "Mexican Labor in Los Angeles." University of California—Los Angeles. Manuscript.

Morgenthau, Tom, et al. 1988. "The Drug Gangs." *Newsweek*, March 28, pp. 20–27.

Mott, Frank L., and R. Jean Haurin. 1988. "Linkages between Sexual Activity and Alcohol and Drug Use among American Adolescents." *Family Planning Perspectives* 20:128–36.

Muller, Thomas, and Thomas J. Espenshade. 1986. *The Fourth Wave*. Washington, D.C.: Urban Institute Press.

Ong, Paul. 1988. "The Hispanization of L.A.'s Poor." University of California—Los Angeles. Photocopy.

Pachon, Harry. 1985. "Overview: Citizenship and the Hispanic Community." In *Proceedings: First National Conference on Citizenship and the Hispanic Community*. Washington, D.C.: National Association of Latino Elected and Appointed Officials.

Padilla, Felix. 1990. "Going to Work: The Entrepreneurial Side of the Gang." Loyola University. Photocopy.

Perkins, Useni Eugene. 1987. *Explosion of Chicago's Black Street Gangs: 1900 to Present*. Chicago: Third World Press.

Pitt, Leonard. 1966. *The Decline of the Californios*. Berkeley, Calif.: University of California Press.

Quicker, John. 1983. *Homegirls: Characterizing Chicana Gangs*. San Pedro, Calif.: International Universities Press.

Reckless, Walter, Simon Dinitz, and B. Kay. 1957. "The Self Component in Potential Delinquency and Potential Non-Delinquency." *American Sociological Review* 22:566–70.

Redfield, Robert. 1941. *Folk Culture of Yucatan*. Chicago: University of Chicago Press.

Reinhold, Robert. 1988. "In the Middle of L.A.'s Gang Warfare." *New York Times Magazine*, May 22, pp. 30–33,66–67,70,74.

Romo, Ricardo. 1983. *East Los Angeles: History of a Barrio.* Austin: University of Texas Press.

Rubel, Arthur. 1965. "The Mexican American Palomilla." *Anthropological Linguistics* 4:92–97.

Salcido, Ramon. 1979. "An Exploratory Sub-Study on the Attitudes, Practice Methods, and Experiences of Gang Workers Who Work with Chicano Gangs." In Joan Moore, *Final Report: A Model for Chicano Drug Use and Effective Utilization of Employment and Training Resources by Barrio Addicts and Ex-Offenders.* Los Angeles: Chicano Pinto Research Project.

Sassen, Saskia. 1988. *The Mobility of Labor and Capital.* Cambridge, Eng.: Cambridge University Press.

Shaw, Clifford, and Henry McKay. 1931. "Social Factors in Juvenile Delinquency." In *National Commission on Law Observance and Enforcement. Report on Causes of Crime,* vol. 2. Washington, D.C.: U.S. Government Printing Office.

————. 1943. *Juvenile Delinquency and Urban Areas.* Chicago: University of Chicago Press.

Short, James. 1990. "New Wine in Old Bottles? Change and Continuity in American Gangs." In *Gangs in America,* edited by C. Ronald Huff. Newbury Park, Calif.: Sage Publications.

Slawson, John. 1926. *The Delinquent Boy.* Boston: Badger Press.

Smith, Douglas. 1964. *Expressed Feelings and Opinions of Adolescent Male Gang Members about One Another and about the Interaction in Their Group.* M.S.W. thesis, University of Southern California.

Soja, Edward, Rebecca Morales, and Goetz Wolff. 1984. "Urban Restructuring: An Analysis of Social and Spatial Change in Los Angeles." *Economic Geography* 59:195–230.

Spergel, Irving. 1986. "The Violent Gang Problem in Chicago: A Local Community Perspective." *Social Service Review* 60:94–131.

Sullivan, Mercer. 1989. *"Getting Paid": Youth Crime and Work in the Inner City.* Ithaca, N.Y.: Cornell University Press.

Suttles, Gerald. 1968. *The Social Order of the Slum.* Chicago: University of Chicago Press.

Sweeney, Terrence. 1980. *Streets of Anger, Streets of Hope: Youth Gangs in East Los Angeles.* Glendale, Calif.: Great Western Publishing.

Taylor, Carl. 1990. *Dangerous Society.* East Lansing, Mich.: Michigan State University Press.

TELACU. 1978. "TELACU: A Framework for Greater East Los Angeles

Industrial Development." Los Angeles: The East Los Angeles Community Union.

Thrasher, Frederick. 1927. *The Gang*. Chicago: University of Chicago Press.

Tienda, Marta, and Leif Jensen. 1988. "Poverty and Minorities: A Quarter Century Profile of Color and Socioeconomic Disadvantage." In *Divided Opportunities*, edited by Gary Sandefur and Marta Tienda. New York: Plenum Press.

U.S. Department of Commerce, Area Redevelopment Administration. 1965. *Hard Core Unemployment and Poverty in Los Angeles*. Washington, D.C.: U.S. Government Printing Office.

Vigil, Diego. 1988a. *Barrio Gangs*. Austin: University of Texas Press.

———. 1988b. "Group Processes and Street Identity: Adolescent Chicano Gang Members." *Ethos* 16:421–45.

———. 1988c. "Street Socialization, Locura Behavior, and Violence among Chicano Gang Members." Jess Kraus, Susan Sorenson, and Paul Juarez, eds. In *Proceedings: Research Conference on Violence and Homicide in Hispanic Communities*, edited by Jess Kraus, Susan Sorenson, and Paul Juarez. Los Angeles: University of California.

———. 1989. "An Emerging Barrio Underclass: Irregular Lifestyles among Former Chicano Gang Members." Working Paper no. 7, New Directions for Latino Public Policy Research. Austin: Center for Mexican American Studies, University of Texas.

Waldorf, Dan. 1980. "A Brief History of Illicit Drug Ethnographies." In *Ethnography: A Research Tool for Policymakers in the Drug and Alcohol Fields*, edited by Carl Akins and George Beschner. Rockville, Md.: National Institute on Drug Abuse.

Warner, W. Lloyd. 1937. *Black Civilization*. New York: Harper.

Werner, Emmy E. 1983. "Vulnerability and Resiliency among Children at Risk for Delinquency." Manuscript.

Williams, Norma. 1989. "The Mexican American Family: Tradition and Change." Manuscript.

Willis, Paul. 1981. *Learning to Labor*. New York: Columbia University Press.

Wilson, Monica. 1951. *Good Company*. London: Oxford University Press.

Wilson, William Julius. 1987. *The Truly Disadvantaged*. Chicago: University of Chicago Press.

Woods, Joseph G. 1973. "The Progressives and the Police: Urban Reform and the Professionalization of the Los Angeles Police." Ph.D. diss., University of California—Los Angeles.

and use of word "gang," 4, 7. *See
also Los Angeles Times*, stories on
gangs; Media
Normal adolescent deviance: and
gang deviance, 131–33; theory of,
39–40

Ohlin, Lloyd, 42, 43
Older gang members, 8; as sources of
drugs, 51, 52
Ong, Paul, 20
"Originals," 140

"Pacific Rim" dominance, 19
Padilla, Felix, 43, 131, 135
Palomillas, 26
Parents of gang members. *See*
Fathers of earlier and recent clique
members; Gang members' families;
Mothers of gang members
Participatory research, 147
Part-time workers, 116
Partying, and getting high, 50–53
Patriarchal families, 84; and in-
cest, 96
PCP, 5, 50, 125, 143; and gang
violence, 66
Perkins, Useni Eugene, 43
Personal problems, of squares, 129
Physically handicapped, 116; and
family problems, 100–101
Physical violence, against children,
93–94
Plea bargaining, by gang members, 5
Police, 151n; and assumptions about
gang drug dealing, 4–5; atti-
tude of toward Stoners, 34–35;
and changes in gangs, 134; and
demise of gang programs, 37–38;
and differences between black and

Chicano gangs, 149–50n; and increased deviance of gangs, 46–47;
and moral panics in American
cities, 1–3; and myth of hereditary
gangs, 49, 114, 153n; and Zoot-
Suit Riots, 151n. *See also* Police
brutality; Police harassment; Police
sweeps in "gang areas"
Police brutality: demonstrations
against, 21; and politicization of
East Los Angeles, 17; and sweeps,
4. *See also* Police harassment
Police harassment: and expulsions
from gangs, 65; and future of
gangs, 135; and street hangouts,
122
Police sweeps in "gang areas", 3–4;
and Chicano gangs, 4
Political activity: in East Los Angeles
after World War II, 15–17; in 1960s
and 1970s, 21
Political representation, 18, 21–22
Polk, Kenneth, 14
Poverty: defined, 151n; in East
Los Angeles and Maravilla in
1980s, 17; of employed Mexican
Americans, blacks, and Anglos
compared, 152n; of full-time
Mexican-American workers, 21;
and household economy during
childhood of gang members, 86,
88–89; and "maladaptive parenting," 81
"Pre-delinquency," 150n
Pregnancy: and girl gang members,
31; parental reaction to, 95. *See
also* Motherhood, gang women and
Prison, 118, 156n; and cholos, 125;
culture, and clique membership,
33; hangouts after, 121–22; and